Jacobean Appliqué

Book I – "EXOTICA"

JACOBEAN APPLIQUÉ

Book I – "EXOTICA"

Patricia B. Campbell & Mimi Ayars, Ph.D.

Photography by Richard Walker, Schenevus, NY

American Quilter's Society
P.O. Box 3290
Paducah, KY 42002-3290

Dedicated to the two Scotsmen in our lives:
DOUG & BRUCE

Every effort has been made to make the instructions in this book
complete and accurate.

For questions about this book and information
about "Exotica" workshops contact:
Patricia B. Campbell
9794 Forest Lane
Suite 900
Dallas, TX 75243

Library of Congress Cataloging-in-Publication Data

Campbell, Patricia.
    Jacobean appliqué / Patricia Campbell and Mimi Ayars; photography by Richard Walker.
        p. cm.
    Contents: Bk. 1. "Exotica".
    ISBN 0-89145-820-4 (v. 1): $18.95
    1. Appliqué – Patterns.   2. Quilting – Patterns.   3. Decoration and ornament,
Jacobean. I. Ayars, Mimi. II. Title.
TT779.C36 1993   93-11934
746.9 '7–dc20   CIP

Additional copies of this book may be ordered from:

American Quilter's Society
P.O. Box 3290
Paducah, KY 42002-3290

@$18.95. Add $1.00 for postage & handling.

TABLE OF CONTENTS

FOREWORD

Friends insisted that I attend a
Pat Campbell workshop. "Come on,
we'll have a good time," they said.
Because I'm a piecer rather than a
patcher, I went reluctantly neither well
prepared nor enthusiastic.

I was impressed, however. Having
taught at the university level all my life,
I knew a good teacher when I saw one.
Furthermore, the quality of Pat's workmanship was not lost on this piecer,
and my friends and I did have a good
time.

When a participant asked Pat if she had
a book and her response was,
"No, but I've been thinking about it,"
my writer mode kicked in. The next day
I wrote to Pat, indicating my interest
in doing a book with her. I enclosed my
credentials and suggested we get
together to talk about the idea.

This book is the result.

— Mimi Ayars, Ph.D.
Author and Illustrator

FOREWORD

One Christmas my mother gave me her lovely silver thimble wrapped in a velvet-lined walnut shell. I cherish this thimble and wish my mother had lived to see how well I can "ply a needle."

Like many quiltmakers, I came to my special niche via a circuitous route — needlepoint canvasses, quilting classes, needlework groups. Then I discovered appliqué.

A move brought me to Dallas, and I joined the quilt guild. I was asked to teach a class on Baltimore Album appliqué. From there it was a short step to Jacobean appliqué.

When Mimi, a quiltmaker and writer, and I met, it was immediate mutual admiration. She admired my skill with the needle; I admired her skill with the pen. You will find her instructions simple and clear. I hope you like our book.

— Patricia B. Campbell
Quilt Artist and Teacher

"You're making a what?" Mary asked Nina as they
walked from the guild meeting to the car.

"A Jacobean quilt."

"What in the world is that?"

"Come on. I'll tell you over lunch."

CHAPTER I — INTRODUCTION

JACOBEAN

Jacobean (Jack´-uh-beé-un) refers to James I, who succeeded Queen Elizabeth to the English throne. This is the James of the King James version of the Bible. It was during James' reign that the colonies at Jamestown and Plymouth were settled. Although "Jacobean" was not coined until 200 years after his rule, it derives from the formal title he called himself: "Jacobus Britanniae Rex."

A more accurate name would have referred to "Stuart," because the so-called "Jacobean" period began with King James, the first of the Stuarts (1603-1625), and ended with Queen Anne, the last of the Stuarts (1702-1714). Architecture, furniture, literature, entertainment, and needlework of a distinctive style reflected the times to such an extent that they can be identified today.

Embroidery associated with James' name has distinguishable characteristics: the Oriental "Tree of Life" with graceful branches and rolling mounds; the Elizabethan scroll with sweeping stems swirling around flowers, a wavy border, oversized leaves with curled or notched edges, and curved blossoms. It was the design, not the stitches, that set this type of stitchery apart from others.

Both pastels and bright colors were used in a naturalistic and stylized manner to portray the flora and fauna of not only England but also distant lands. Colors ranged from deep green to contrasting rose, purple, blue, and gold. Glorious shading was used to give dimension. It is generally thought that the colors were muted, but perhaps it has been time rather that the maker that mellowed them.

The exotic Jacobean needlework, generally called "crewel," was made of soft, slackly twisted, two-ply worsted yarn worked with a needle on linen. Wall and bed hangings were cherished and passed from one generation to the next with great pride. Table covers, chair seats, and bedspreads were other household items decorated with Jacobean stitchery.

British immigrants brought some of their treasures with them when they came to the colonies. A few New England embroiderers kept the art from dying. In America "crewel" (spelled many different ways) has been the name preferred over "Jacobean." The designs were adapted to American taste. They were less busy than the old designs with greater variety and more unadorned background. Realistic designs, reflective of everyday American life, replaced the fantasy ones. There was a lightness, a vitality, a gaiety unlike the English counterpart: a freedom of spirit, unique to the new land.

APPLIQUÉ

The word "appliqué," taken from the Latin "applicare" meaning "to fasten to," comes to English via the French, adopted whole-cloth, even to the accent mark on the "e."

Appliqué is probably as old as humanity, and seems to be universal. From the Eskimos' decorating their skins with other skins to East Indians' attaching mirrors to cotton, from Siberia to Peru, possessions are repaired and/or embellished through applying pieces. Although appliqué can refer to applying any material onto any other material in any manner, it has come to mean, especially to quiltmakers, stitching one fabric piece onto the surface of another fabric piece. In earlier times this technique was called "laid-on" work or "patchwork."

JACOBEAN APPLIQUÉ

A new quilt art form was created when Pat Campbell started adapting old Jacobean embroidery designs for new Jacobean appliqué designs. She talked with friends, searched local libraries and antiquarian book shops for information, and visited museums in England.

Her first quilt top, "Jacobean Arbor," the well-known and beloved black quilt, with its colorful and graceful stems, leaves, berries, flowers, and vines, is stitched with perfection. "Elizabethan Woods" followed. These spectacular and multi-award winning quilts have appeared on the covers of American Quilter (1990), Patchwork Quilt Tsushin (1991), and Quilting International (1992). Articles have featured them in Quilting Today (1991), American Quilter (1990), and International Quilt Festival (1991).

Today, this internationally known artist and teacher adapts patterns, designs quilt tops, and shows others the joy of Jacobean Appliqué. "Exotica" was designed especially for you.

"I never met a quilter," said Nina, "who didn't adore fabric. We buy it; we stockpile it; we brag about it. And as soon as we cut into a piece, we run out and buy more to replace it."

Chapter II — Get Ready

FABRICS

You'll find only a few rules in this book. Rather than "thou shalt nots," consider them strong recommendations to keep you off "rocky shoals."

Rule Number 1: Use 100% cotton fabrics.

Why? They are easier to needle turn. If you don't know whether a piece of fabric in your collection is all-cotton or a blend, do a simple test. Cut off a small piece, put it in an ashtray, and set it on fire. If only ashes of the "blow-away" type remain, the swatch was cotton. If it melts, polyester (part of the blend) was present.

BACKGROUND FABRIC (BF)

A Jacobean quilt has background fabric, which will henceforth be abbreviated "BF," and design fabric, henceforth abbreviated "DF."

First, let's discuss background fabric (BF). Traditional quiltmakers are inclined to think "muslin," because it has been so widely used for such a long time. Our forebears had little choice; their heirs have many choices. White, off-white, beige, eggshell, chamois, tan, and black — all neutrals — permit a wide array of fabrics and colors to be used for the appliquéd design. Other background colors are limiting.

Rule Number 2: Always buy good BF.

When you're shopping, examine the fabric weave. It must be straight and even. It may be expensive. But this is a poor place to economize. You're investing many hours of your life in this masterpiece, and you don't want it ruined by bargain fabric.

Try to avoid buying material that has been torn. Tearing bruises, stretches, and weakens the fabric, requiring that part of it be cut off. This means you have to allow for the waste. Ask that your fabric be cut.

Gutcheon's "American Classic" is excellent quality and comes in many beautiful colors; the dye doesn't change from one lot to the next. Yes, it ravels, because it is perfectly on grain. Zigzag or cut with pinking shears to minimize the raveling. You will trim this away later.

Four yards of fabric are needed for the background of "Exotica." If you want to make the back of the quilt the same fabric, you will need four additional yards.

DESIGN FABRIC (DF)

If you, like most quiltmakers, adore fabric and horde it, now is the time to go through your treasure chest and choose those fabrics you'd like to use for your design pieces.

Traditional Jacobean colors are greens, indigo blues, browns, and roses. They are soft and blended colors, never startling, but jewel-like. You don't need to be locked into that tradition. Leaves and tree trunks can be done realistically in greens and browns, but flowers can be pure fantasy. Don't worry about your wallhanging's not fitting the decor of the room where you want to display it. As with most quilts, a Jacobean quilt will go with anything anywhere.

Choose some small prints and some large prints. The popular multicolored calicoes in their busyness distract from the unity of the total design. A calico with five, six, or seven colors pushes people to blend, match or coordinate. Two-color or shaded calicoes give more freedom. RJR Fashion Fabrics has an excellent selection.

Hand-dyed fabrics, usually sold in fat quarters, add interest. Try Skydyes. Tropical prints with oversized flowers and leaves, although multicolored, can be a great source for brilliant highlights and leaf treatment. Look at the Alexander Henry and Hoffman collections.

If you use see-through templates, they can be placed over the exact section of the fabric design you want. Don't be afraid to make Swiss cheese out of a piece of fabric to get those parts you like. For example, cut a small leaf to be appliquéd from a large printed leaf and have the veins in place. Baltimore Album quiltmakers had to embroider veins on their leaves.

Be cautious about using plain colored fabrics. They tend to give a "flat" look, whereas prints, with their textured appearance, give depth. If you decide to use solids, stay with them; don't bring in two or three calicoes; they would be distracting. Pastels are okay, if there are also darker shades for contrast.

Some fabrics will be used throughout the quilt, such as the greens and browns for tree trunks and stems. Others used to add sparkle, excitement, and action appear only here and there. Sparkle colors are lipstick red, poison green (yellow around the gills), hot pink, mustard yellow, burnt orange, electric blue, and dazzling purple. Exciting and action prints are those with strong contrast; they have feeling and bring your quilt to life. Keep in mind, however, that you want an exciting experience, not a wild party.

Variety is the spice of life in Jacobean designs. How do you get variety? Cruise the quilt shops and fabric stores in your area, but be very discriminating in your selection. Buy fat quarters. Share with friends. Trade at your bee or guild. Invite a group to make a wallhanging with you and pool your fabrics. Even if you all use the same fabrics, each finished quilt will be different, for it will have the maker's personal stamp on it.

Appliqué permits more freedom in use of color than you have experienced in piecing, but if you are timid about color combinations, use the book's photos as a guide. When you have completed "Exotica," you will have more confidence in expressing your sense of color.

Other materials you'll need are fabric for the backing of the quilt, fabric for the sleeve, batting, and squares of Pellon® or muslin for laying out your pieces and making your sewing project portable.

THREAD

Machine embroidery thread is thinner than regular sewing thread and hides well. You will need an array of shades. A group of friends working on Jacobean quilts can pool their thread, increasing the choices and decreasing the expense. If you can't match a particular piece exactly, go a shade darker, not a shade lighter.

Choose quilting thread the color of your background, so your quilting doesn't compete with your design.

TOOLS

You will need a number of tools. Some you "gotta have" and some you "wanna have." Check off the ones you already have.

"GOTTA HAVES"

■ *Scissors: Template cutting, fabric cutting*

You must have two kinds, one for cutting templates and one for cutting fabric. Don't ruin your sharp fabric scissors by cutting paper or plastic with them. The Fiskars™ 5" Sharp Point is great for templates. Gingher™ 4" embroidery scissors work well for design pieces.

■ *Needles: #12 Betweens*

Just as you can get a small stitch in quilting with a thin short needle, you can get a small stitch for your appliqué with a thin short needle. The shorter, the stronger! A long needle (for example, a milliner's or a so-called appliqué needle, #7-11 sharp) is hard to control. It wiggles and bends and makes needle turning hard. Though the eye of a #12 is small, the thread is thin. Therefore, the needle is not hard to thread. Experiment with the Clover® brand.

■ *Pencils: Silver, white, mechanical lead*

Silver and white pencils for dark fabrics, and a mechanical lead one for light fabrics are all you need. Berol™ Prisma Color® pencils work well, though their very soft lead breaks easily. A mechanical pencil always has a sharp point.

A yellow pencil marks well on dark fabrics,

but its wax base melts when heat hits it, so don't use yellow where you don't want yellow to show later.

■ Eraser

Any kind of eraser can be used. If you follow the instructions, you're not going to have many marks to remove. If you need to buy an eraser, try Pentel™ Clic®.

■ Pins: Glass headed, quilting, Sashiko, sequin (sometimes called "appliqué" pins)

Glass-headed and quilting pins are easy to see and pretty. They are also easy to find in the carpet if you want to protect family members and pets. Sashiko pins (Japanese) are very sharp and have a tendency to attack. Treat them with respect. You'll be giving inspiration and perspiration to this quilt; you don't want to be a blood donor, too. Should an accident occur, moisten a small wad of quilting thread with saliva and dab it on the fresh blood. The thread will absorb the blood, removing the stain.

Sequin pins are short. They are great for not getting in your way, but often they are thick and their bluntness tends to bruise the fabric. Look for sequin pins that are marked "appliqué" pins; they tend to be a little less blunt. Be careful where you use them. Remember thin pins make little holes; fat pins make big holes.

■ Light box

A light box is essential for tracing a pattern on a dark background, and it makes transferring a pattern to a light background easier, too. You can purchase a light box, which is not inexpensive, or you can improvise.

Taping your pattern to a window and holding background fabric over it permits you to trace the pattern easily. Any glass top table with a lamp set under it works fine, too. A table with leaves can be pulled apart and a plastic desktop protector laid across the space. With a lamp under it you see well and mark with ease.

■ Sandpaper board

Quiltmakers collect gadgets – some are used rarely, others often. A sandpaper board is one that will be used again and again, to keep fabric from slipping when you're marking.

You can purchase a board in a number of sizes. Some are fancy and expensive. You can make your own inexpensively. A sheet of fine sandpaper glued to a piece of plywood or heavy cardboard works exactly like the commercial ones. A sheet glued to the inside of a manila file folder makes a portable sandpaper board.

■ Pens: Permanent, washable

A pen is needed to mark plastic templates. Some inks can be washed off. A Sharpie™ pen is permanent. If you like a dark edge on your templates, use it. If you prefer a clear template, use a pen with washable ink and sponge the lines off after cutting it out. Of course, a pencil can be used and the lines then erased for a clear template. Experiment to see which you like.

■ *Template material: Template plastic, laminate plastic, clear Contact™ paper, medical paper, freezer paper*

You need only one type of template material. Choose whichever is available. 13" x 20" template plastic is a good size and can be purchased in quilt shops. Clear-Adheer™, "do-it-yourself-laminate" packaged with 50 sheets, or clear Contact™ paper can be used over a duplicated copy. Medical paper used on examining tables is strong and translucent. Of course, there is always freezer paper.

■ *Thimble*

The needle you'll be using is so fine that the eye end can easily puncture your finger. Consider a thimble as "armor" against injury.

■ *Lamp*

Any good lamp will do, but a gooseneck or swing-arm helps to direct the light on your work. A halogen bulb (72 watts), being cooler than a regular bulb, will make working more pleasant.

■ *Pincushion*
■ *Ruler*
■ *Iron and board*
■ *Sewing machine*
■ *Comfortable chair*
■ *Eye glasses*

You cannot do without a sewing machine, ruler, iron, good glasses, excellent light, and comfortable chair.

"WANNA HAVES"

■ *Scissors: pinking shears*

Pinking shears can be used to cut background fabric edges to avoid raveling, making machine zigzag stitching unnecessary.

■ *Rotary cutter and pad*

A rotary cutter and pad can be used so extensively by a quiltmaker that they are not a luxury. These items may be "gotta haves" for you.

■ *T-square*

When you are making your background blocks, a T-square is very useful. If you don't have one, there are other ways to see that the blocks are square. These are explained in a later chapter.

ILLUSTRATIONS IN THIS BOOK

Each block is shown with a color photograph, a full-size master pattern in quadrants and full-size templates. The border pieces are shown in either eight or ten sections (depending on their length) with full-size master patterns, and full-size templates. These, plus figures and detailed instructions, will help you make your own heirloom quilt.

Unlike sewing patterns that use "_ _ _" to indicate sewing lines and "____" to indicate cutting lines, the illustrations in this book reverse them because when you trace a template you make a solid line.

"I'd like to make a Jacobean quilt, like Nina," Mary announced to two friends. "Wouldn't you?"

"Yes, we could share fabric and supplies," offered Sandy.

"We'd then have a wide assortment and less expense," suggested Kate.

"Great idea," they agreed. "Let's!"

CHAPTER III — GET SET

GATHERING FABRICS

Gather the fabrics you think you'll use. Keep in mind you're looking for 100% cotton content, variety of print size and shades, contrast and sparkle colors.

First, choose your background fabric (BF). A light shade is recommended. Second, decide which fabrics will be used throughout the nine blocks and border. Third, which other pieces will you use?

Plan one block at a time. After four or five blocks have been stitched, choose some fabrics from these blocks to use in the remaining blocks. Also, choose some fabrics that have not been used. The "new" fabrics will give the blocks a special interest of their own; the "old" fabrics will maintain unity when the completed top is viewed as a whole.

CUTTING BLOCKS AND BORDERS

Cut away the selvage from your background fabric (BF). Then cut nine blocks 16" x 16", two borders 11" x 47", two borders 11" x 67", and two strips for binding 1" x 144". To insure that all pieces are square, use a T-square or a ruler and the lines on your cutting pad. If you follow Fig. 1, you'll avoid the center fold mark on your fabric.

All the pieces must be cut from the yardage in the same direction. Mixing cross-cut pieces with lengthwise cut pieces and/or reversing pieces can cause a difference in appearance in terms of texture, shading, or sheen. You want the background to look the same all over the quilt top. To avoid rotating the pieces, tag each as you cut by stitching a little square of paper in the upper right-hand corner. On it mark: "N" (for North), an arrow pointing up, and the Block number. Fig. 2.

Tag each border piece as you did the blocks, with "N" (for North), an arrow pointing up, and the position — "top," "bottom," "left," "right." Fig. 3. Notice that the top and bottom borders are tagged on the left rather than the right; also notice the direction of the arrow on those pieces.

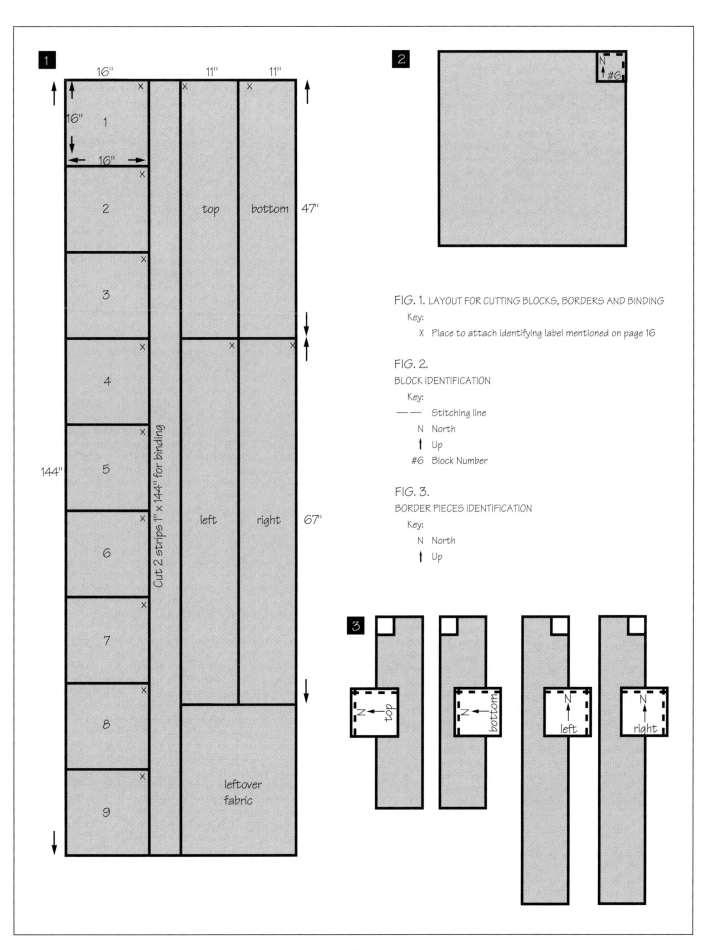

1

16"   11"   11"

16"

1

16"

2   top   bottom   47"

3

4

Cut 2 strips 1" x 144" for binding

5

144"

6   left   right   67"

7

8

leftover
fabric

9

2

N
↑ #6

FIG. 1. LAYOUT FOR CUTTING BLOCKS, BORDERS AND BINDING
  Key:
    X   Place to attach identifying label mentioned on page 16

FIG. 2.
BLOCK IDENTIFICATION
  Key:
  — —   Stitching line
    N   North
    ↑   Up
    #6   Block Number

FIG. 3.
BORDER PIECES IDENTIFICATION
  Key:
    N   North
    ↑   Up

3

N ← top   N ← bottom   N left   N right

Cut nine freezer paper or tracing paper squares 15" x 15", two strips 10" x 45", and two strips 10" x 65".

Cut the ends of the two binding strips (1" x 144") on a perfect 45° angle so they are ready for sewing. Lay them aside for later, having tagged the right side. If you bought an extra four yards of your BF for backing, put it aside.

A straight, even weave ravels easily, so pink or zigzag all the raw edges, except the binding strips. Avoid serging; it tends to draw up the fabric. These edges will be trimmed after the blocks and borders are sewn together.

MAKING A MASTER PATTERN

On one of the squares, trace with a felt tip pen the quadrants of the full-size pattern for Block #1, lining them up on the dotted lines and marked centers. This will be your master pattern for Block #1. Be sure to mark in red the letters, and the asterisk as shown on page 41. As you stitch, you'll want to keep the master handy for reference. Go through the same steps for the other blocks and the border pieces.

Also cut nine "portable" Pellon® or muslin blocks 18" x 18", two strips 12" x 48", and two strips 12" x 68". Their use will also be explained later. These can be reused for future projects.

To help you get started: only Block #1 has letters as well as numbers on the master pattern. The numbers are for identification, but not sequence. However, the letters do indicate the sequence order in which the pieces should be stitched. Patterns for the other blocks and the border pieces do not show letters. After completing one block you will have a "feel" for the stitching order.

MARKING PATTERN
ON BACKGROUND FABRIC

Now you're ready to trace the pattern on the BF of your Block #1. Indicate the center of the block by folding the square in half, then in half in the other direction. Pinch the center point. Fig. 4. Do not mark the center with pen or pencil in case your design doesn't cover that spot.

Tape your master pattern to a flat surface. Center a BF block over it. Be sure to match your master pattern center with your block center and square your pattern with your block. You can easily see through light colored fabric. Use a light box if you have a dark background.

Mark the lines on the BF about ⅛" to ¼" inside the pattern line to suggest where the pieces go. A single line can serve for the tree trunk and each stem. Put an "X" where you will place the small pieces.

You will have more freedom if there is no pencil line to follow exactly. The precision of piecing is not needed in appliqué, because one piece is stitched at a time. If the piece is slightly off and

4

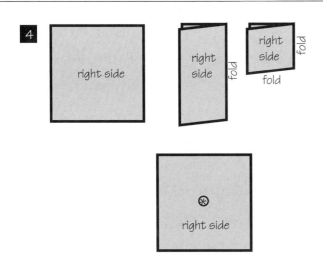

FIG. 4. MARKING THE CENTER OF THE BLOCK
Key:
 ⊙ Center

FIG. 5. MARKING THE CENTER OF THE BORDER
Key:
 ⊙ Center

5

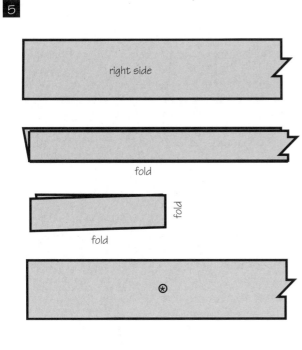

you have a minimum of background markings, you won't need to remove pencil marks later.

Repeat for the other blocks. Follow the same steps for the border pieces; fold in half lengthwise and then in half crosswise. Pinch the middle. Fig. 5. Tape the border strip master pattern to a flat surface. Center the BF border strip over it, square the two pieces, and mark as you did with the blocks.

MARKING AND CUTTING TEMPLATES

With a Sharpie™ pen (if you want your lines to be permanent) or with a template marking pencil or a lead pencil (if you want to remove the marks and have a clear template), trace the template patterns on plastic just as they appear in the book. With a permanent marker identify each with its block number (#1, #2, #3, #4, #5, #6, #7, #8, #9) and piece number (1, 2, 3, 4, 5, 6, etc.). Fig. 6. The piece numbers do not refer to the order of stitching; they are for identification only.

6

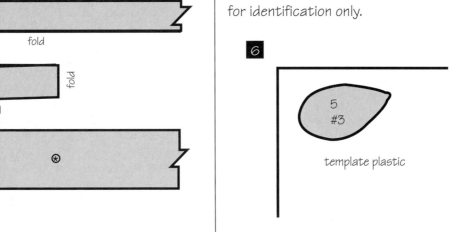

FIG. 6. TEMPLATE IDENTIFICATION
Key:
 5 template number
   for block
 3 block number

You want to draw perfect circles, cut perfect circles, and stitch perfect circles, so a perfect template is the first step. When you cut out the plastic circle, make sure it is perfectly round. If it isn't, smooth the little jags with an emery board.

Some tree trunk templates are too big to fit on the book page; for example, in Blocks #2, #5, and #6. These have been split and marked A_____B. Of course, you will make one template of the two pieces.

Block templates follow the block master pattern quadrants which start on page 42. Border templates are at the end of the border master pattern sections on page 152.

Cut out all of your templates. Store them in plastic bags with the templates of each block in a separate bag marked with the block number. Pin the bag to the master pattern for that block.

MARKING AND CUTTING DESIGN PIECES

Start with Block #1. Lay the fabric right side up on your sandpaper board to keep it from slipping while you mark. Hold the pencil at an angle with the top tipped away from the template so that the point angles into the template. This lets you mark close to the template and keeps the point sharp. These marks will disappear when you needle turn. Continue with the other pieces for that block.

Don't hesitate to use a printed leaf for your leaf piece, cutting a small appliqué leaf from a large printed one. Place the template so that the printed veins become the veins of your leaf. This is the advantage of using see-through templates. Cut the leaf out, bringing the cutting line out to a point. There is no need to blunt cut the end. Keep the tips pointed as in Fig. 7.

Unlike sewing patterns that use a broken line to indicate sewing lines and a solid line to indicate cutting lines, the illustrations in this book reverse them because when you trace the template you make a solid line.

On the inside of the tulip there is a straight edge and a scalloped edge. You'll notice that the space between these two edges on the template pattern allows for only one seam allowance, not

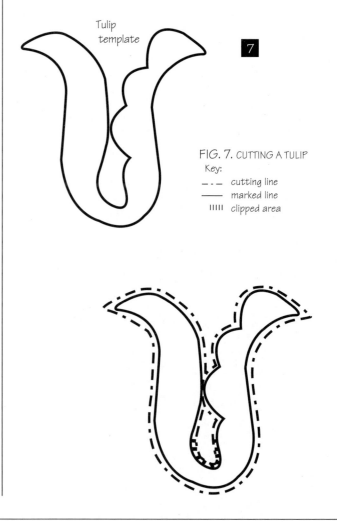

Tulip template

7

FIG. 7. CUTTING A TULIP

Key:
‒ · ‒   cutting line
─────   marked line
||||| clipped area

two. Cut the fabric so that the allowance is all on the scalloped side and there is no allowance for a short space (about ½") on the straight side. Fig. 7. When you stitch, you will overlap, hiding the raw edge.

There is an ongoing argument among appliqué teachers regarding cutting pieces on the straight or bias. Some judges insist that every appliquéd piece must be on the grain of the BF. Some appliqué teachers wonder if these judges themselves appliqué. Putting the design piece on its straight is handicap enough, but having to put it on the straight of the BF is a double handicap.

Demonstrate to yourself whether you want your pieces on the straight or the bias. Cut a small oval. Locate the grain. Where will the most ravel be? On the straight! Every straight grain ravels. Where will the least ravel be? On the bias! Compare the areas of most and least ravel on each of the ovals in Fig. 8. "B" will ravel less easily than "A" and will be much easier to needle turn. Grain going

a number of different ways lends interest.

Add ⅛" seam allowance to your template marking when you cut (yes, ⅛" – don't faint). Fig. 9. If you can't bring yourself to allow such a tiny amount, cut ¼" and then when you're ready to appliqué, cut the allowance in half. This, of course, will waste time and fabric.

As you cut each piece out, position it on your BF square. When all the pieces are placed, look at your block in terms of color and contrast. Squint your eyes. Try the blocks in different lighting. Does any one piece jump out or fade? Do all the pieces appeal to you? If not, remove those that offend. When you are happy with your choices, carefully remove the pieces and lay them in the approximate position on your portable blocks. Pin them in place.

8

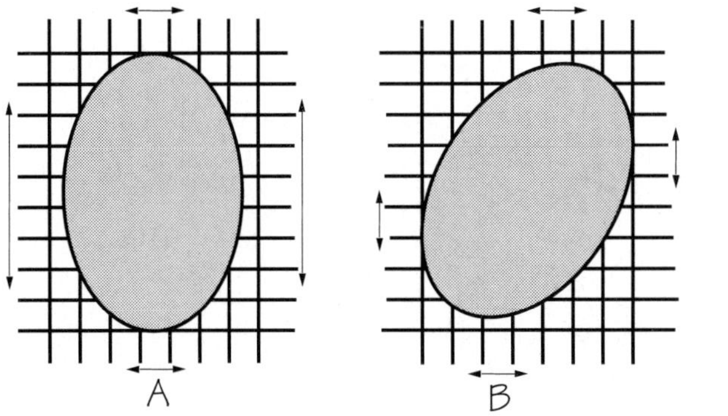

FIG. 8. AREAS OF MOST AND LEAST RAVEL
Key:
    A On straight
    B On bias
    ↔ Indicates area size of potential ravel

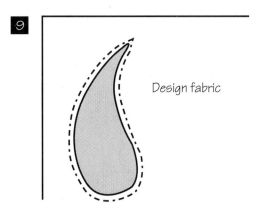

FIG. 9. MARKING AND CUTTING LINES FOR DESIGN FABRIC PIECES
Key:
   –·– Cutting line for 1/8" seam allowance
   ___ Marked template line

Design fabric

"Are we having fun yet?" asked Sandy in the voice of a child on a trip.

"I am," announced Kate, as she fingered Mary's material. *"Me, too,"* the others chorused.

"But wait till we come to the stitching," said Nina. *"The Campbell secrets make it not only fun but also easy."*

"Maybe they're the same thing," the four agreed.

CHAPTER IV — GO

THE CAMPBELL SECRETS

Have the following items handy: #1 BF block, needle(s), pins, master pattern, scissors, thimble, "portable" block with DF pieces, and matching threads.

RULE NUMBER 5:

MATCH THE THREAD TO THE DESIGN FABRIC, NOT THE BACKGROUND FABRIC.

If you don't have the exact shade, go one shade darker, never lighter.

Seat yourself in a comfortable chair with your feet up. This position makes you lean back, not forward – a more relaxed position for stitching. You can hold your piece loosely in your lap or use a pillow or lapboard under it. To maintain a comfortable position that will allow many hours of stitching time, the thumb of the hand holding the background fabric must always face the thumb of the stitching hand. Fig. 10. Don't twist your holding hand; that will hunch up your shoulder, causing fatigue.

Place a good light at your elbow, left side if you're right handed; right side if left handed.

"Vanity, vanity, thy name is vanity." Resist being vain while you work so you can be vain with the results. If you can't see, you can't stitch. Wear glasses if you have them. If you don't wear glasses but find yourself squinting, have your eyes examined.

10

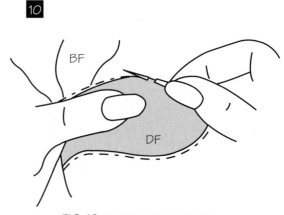

FIG. 10. CORRECT HAND POSITION

Key:
--- cut edge
___ marked line

BASTING

Generally, you can pin baste by placing a few pins here and there on the underside of the block, out of your way. This permits you to stitch without catching the thread. After the piece is partly stitched, the pins can be removed. If you use sequin pins, be careful to separate, not split, the threads of the fabric; these pins are thicker than sashiko, quilt, or glass-headed pins. You probably will want to thread baste tree trunks, because the shifting of such large pieces can be serious.

STITCHING

STARTING

Start by cutting a matching thread (matching DF piece, not BF) 15"-18" long. Mettler® #60 and DMC® #50 are recommended, because they are thin and hide well. Always cut, thread your needle (#12 Between), and knot the same end — that which comes off the spool last. This practice will keep your thread from twisting as you stitch.

Use any knot you like: the one your mama taught you — wetting your first two fingers and twisting (which some people can't do) or the "wrap-around-the needle" quilter's knot (which some people can't do, either). Want to learn one? Make a loop of the thread and hold it with your free thumb and forefinger. Slip the needle through the loop from underneath, twist the thread three times around the needle as if you were making a French knot. Keeping a taut loop,

slide the needle through the loop and slowly pull the thread until only a knot remains in your fingers. Fig. 11. Of course, you can do your own secret knot. The point is that any good clean knot will do.

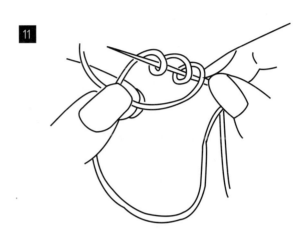

FIG. 11. "WRAP-AROUND-THE-NEEDLE" KNOT

The easiest place to start stitching is on a "straight-away" or on a gentle curve. The asterisk on the Block #1 master pattern indicates a good starting place. By the time you're ready to start the next block, you'll have a feel for where to stitch first.

RULE NUMBER 6:

NEVER START STITCHING AT A POINT.

Anchor your knot under the marked seam allowance of the DF. The knot will then be hidden in the fold. Stitch counterclockwise. This means the seam allowance is away from you, not toward you. Your thumb holding the piece is directly beneath your stitching. Fig. 12.

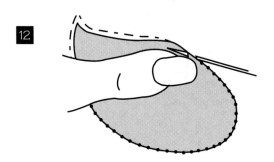

FIG. 12. THUMB DIRECTLY BELOW STITCHING LINE

Key:
– – — Cut edge
_____ Marked line
. . . . . Stitched area

The order in which you stitch the pieces doesn't matter except where pieces overlap. For those pieces, make arrows that show the pieces that go under and the pieces that go over. The shaft of the arrow will be the "under" piece; the arrow head will be the "over" piece. Mark the arrows on your master pattern. Fig. 13. Jumping around on your block rather than concentrating on one area makes the stitching more exciting. Consider doing all the "under" pieces of that block first, so you won't forget later.

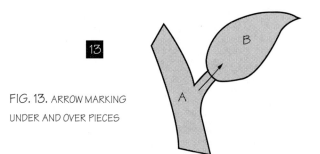

FIG. 13. ARROW MARKING UNDER AND OVER PIECES

If the master pattern is readily at hand, you can check on the order and positioning. Keep in mind, however, in appliqué you don't have to be as exact as you would if you were making a Mariner's Compass block. If you're slightly off, appliqué is forgiving.

Mark arrows on your first few block or border master patterns. Decide where the arrows should go. Mark them on your master pattern before starting to stitch that block or border piece. By the time you finish these first few sections you may not need guidelines. Just continue marking arrows as long as you feel you need them for guidance.

NEEDLE TURNING

Since you use only a little bit of the needle for both turning and stitching, you don't need much of a needle. Shorter is stronger. Try a #12 Between faithfully for a week. New stitchers report they like it better than the so-called appliqué needle. If a #12 is not comfortable, try a #10 Between. Experiment until you find a size you like. Always sew with what is comfortable for you — not with what you're told is the "right" needle.

With the tip of your needle about ¾" from where the thread comes up in the fold, sweep the needle toward you, turning the seam allowance under. Take several stitches and repeat. This technique eliminates pressing or basting. With all the time you save you can make your next Jacobean quilt.

THE STITCH

The stitch you do is a petite version of the hemming stitch you probably learned in a home economics class in high school, but don't take any back stitches, as you likely were taught, because they'll show. Directly out from where your needle emerges on the marked line and slightly under the fold of your DF, put your needle point into the BF, pick up two to three threads and come up into the DF on the marked line (which is the fold) about 1/16" from the last stitch. The picking up of the threads and the emergence into the fold are one motion. Fig. 14.

FIG. 14. NEEDLE POSITION FOR STITCH
Key:
–– Cut edge
——— Marked line
..... Stitched area

Repeat: drop your needle barely under the DF, so the thread disappears. Continue: pick up two to three threads, come up into the fold from underneath, needle turn, pick up two to three threads, come up into the fold, needle turn.

To avoid discomfort in your wrists and shoulders, be sure your thumbs keep facing toward each other.

If you take a stitch too far out from the design piece into the BF, the thread will show. If you take it too deeply into the DF, it will show.

Make your stitch perpendicular to the edge of the design piece. This will line up the stitches. The arrows in Fig. 15 suggest the angle you will be stitching, not the distance from the fold. If your stitches slant, they will not only show, but also dimple the fabric. Try not to make stitches too tight, because the thread will fray and the design piece will ripple.

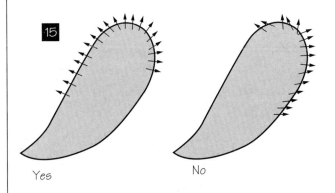

Yes   No

FIG. 15. DIRECTION OF STITCHES

STOPPING

When your thread grows too short to continue, put the needle through to the back of the BF, in from the edge of the design piece. Take a little "bite" of the fabric with the needle. Make a loop of the thread and hold it under your thumb as you gently pull the stitch in place. Fig. 16, Step 1. Repeat with a second "bite." Fig. 16, Step 2.

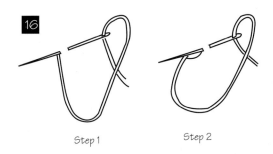

Step 1   Step 2

FIG. 16. FINISHING OFF KNOT

Bury the tail by passing the needle between the two layers (BF and DF) away from the edge. Snip the tail close to the BF so there are no loose threads.

Cut a new piece of thread and knot it. Start with the needle point coming up at the seam allowance mark, very close to the last stitch. The new knot will be hidden in the fold. Proceed as before.

After the piece is appliquéd, end as you did when you ran out of thread. Put the needle through to the back of the BF. Take a tiny bite of fabric making a circle with the thread. Holding the thread under your thumb, pull it up smoothly., Repeat with another bite. Work the tail back in between BF and DF. You don't want any loose threads showing through the background fabric.

PERFECT POINTS

Points are a test for the appliquér. You've probably heard of a number of methods to make a point: fold across the tip and then fold under the seam allowance on each side; use freezer paper and iron seam allowance under; when all else fails, cut the end off to make it less sharp. None of these is recommended.

The "perfect point" method will give you such pretty points that people will think you're an experienced appliquér even if you aren't. The instructions may sound complicated, but if you follow step by step, you'll be delighted with the results.

■ Stitch to the marked point, not to the end of the fabric, but to the marked point — the point where you start down the other side. Fig. 17, Step 1.

■ Take second stitch on top of the last stitch (in the exact same spot) to secure that stitch.

■ Take your thimble off and set your threaded needle in the BF, out of the way.

■ Turn your block as if you were going to start stitching down the other side.

■ Clip off any little tail from the first side seam allowance that noses out. Fig. 17, Step 2.

■ Hold the stitch at the point and the thread firmly under your thumb.

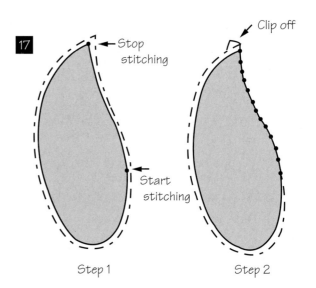

FIG. 17. STITCHING "PERFECT POINTS"
Key:
– – – Cut edge
_____ Marked line
. . . . . Stitched area

■ With a quilter's pin grasped about ½" up from the point and braced from behind with your middle finger to strengthen it (remember shorter is stronger), sweep the seam allowance under from right to left. Then sweep it back from left to right, all the time holding the point tightly with your thumb, lifting it only when you sweep the fabric under. If you don't like the result, pull the seam allowance out with your needle, and try again. Sweep right to left and then left to right.

Sometimes the point frays and workshop participants panic. Don't let fraying intimidate you. The remaining threads are your seam allowance. Just sweep them under and stitch.

■ Still holding the point tightly with your thumb, turn the block so you can take a stitch into the BF about ¹⁄₁₆" out from the fold. Fig. 18.

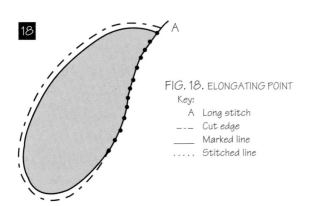

FIG. 18. ELONGATING POINT
Key:
A   Long stitch
–·–   Cut edge
____ Marked line
····· Stitched line

Unlike your other stitches, which you've been trying to hide, you now want this one to show. That extra stitch elongates the point. It will give the illusion that the tip is more pointed than it really is. Proceed with stitching down the other side.

When the appliquéd piece is finished, use your needle to shape the point and use your thumbnail to iron it. "Is that steam or dry iron?" asked a would-be clown in a workshop. "Depends on the humidity!" was the quick retort.

After a week of using this point technique you'll be making sharp points without even thinking about it. The quilter's pin is the tool, but the real secret is the ⅛" seam allowance.

Sometimes there are skinny leaves and sharp points at the end of slender tendrils. All the leaves in "Exotica" are plump, but there are skinny tendril tips in the border. Since you'll be appliquéing them after you've had a great deal of practice with "perfect points," you'll have no problem.

■ Proceed as you did with "perfect points," stitching to the marked point.

■ Take another stitch on top of the last stitch to secure it.

■ Turn the stem back on itself and trim away any excess seam allowance near the point on the side you've just stitched. Also, clip away any loose threads and anything else that will be a hindrance or add bulk.

■ Hold your thumb on the last stitch with the thread under your thumb, out of the way of your stitching. With your quilt pin, sweep right to left and then left to right.

■ Make an elongating stitch at the point.

■ Turn and proceed down the other side.

You probably realize by now that "points with skinny tips are hard" is a myth.

CURVES

Convex

Convex curves (outside curves) are the easiest. Fig. 19. After you have stitched the tree trunk, choose a piece to appliqué that has a gentle convex curve. Your work on this curve will be good even if this is your first appliqué. You don't need to clip, because the seam allowance is only ⅛", rather than ¼".

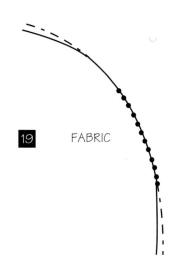

FABRIC

FIG. 19. CONVEX CURVE
Key:
– – – Cut edge
_____ Needle turned area & marked line
. . . . . Stitched area

Concave

Concave curves (inside curves) are a little harder. Clip only when absolutely necessary, which will be rarely, because you have ⅛" seam allowance instead of the usual ¼". Fig. 20. You'll know when you need to clip because you'll feel a drag on the needle or the fold won't stay folded.

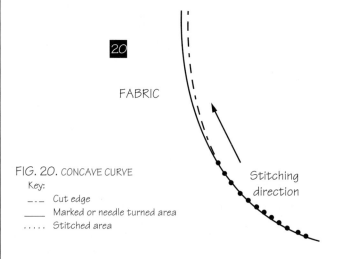

FABRIC

FIG. 20. CONCAVE CURVE
Key:
– – – Cut edge
_____ Marked or needle turned area
. . . . . Stitched area

Stitching direction

When there are two curves – a convex and a concave one, as in a branch, do the concave (inside) first and then the convex (outside). Fig. 21. If the outside is done first, the inside tends to pucker or gather.

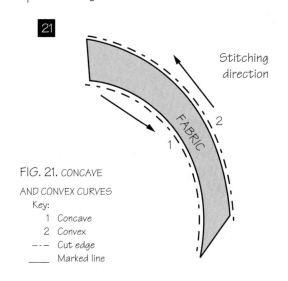

Stitching direction

FABRIC

FIG. 21. CONCAVE
AND CONVEX CURVES
Key:
    1 Concave
    2 Convex
– – – Cut edge
_____ Marked line

"U" Curves

You should have no problem with a "U" if you clip every ⅛" in the seam allowance of the curve before starting to stitch. Fig. 22.

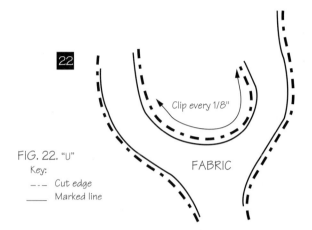

FIG. 22. "U"
Key:
--- Cut edge
___ Marked line

Deep "V"

Clip the "V" to the marked line. If you clip too deeply into the fabric, don't worry. Just make the "V" a little deeper. Stitch to the clip. Flip down the loose side of the piece. Fig. 23. Take a stitch. When you flip it back, the seam allowance on the flipped part turns under, ready for you to continue stitching. The last stitch is taken in the seam allowance, so when the edge is flipped back it positions itself.

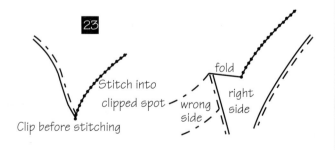

FIG. 23. DEEP "V"
Key:
--- Cut edge
___ Marked line
.... Stitched area

There is little new in needlework. One workshop participant said that when she was young her great-grandmother taught her about flipping down the second side of the "V."

Try a heart like the one in Fig. 24 for practice. In that one piece you'll do a "straight-away" (a), a gentle curve (b), a "deep V" (c), and a "perfect point" (d).

FIG. 24. HEART PRACTICE
Key:
a "Straight away"
b Gentle curve
c Deep "V"
d "Perfect point"

Circles

You'll have perfect circles if they're: 1) marked perfectly, 2) cut perfectly, and 3) sewn perfectly. You've already marked and cut perfect circles. Now you'll stitch perfect circles. Use a pin on the underside to hold the circle in place. Do not clip the seam allowance. Needle turn only enough to take one stitch. Turning under only enough for a single stitch creates a smooth curve; turning under more will create points or a straight line. Take one stitch, turn the circle, needle turn, take one stitch, turn the circle, etc.

Tulips

Clip the "U" at the inside bottom of the tulip every 1/8". Pin the side that has the straight inside edge. (Remember, put pins on the back, so they are out of the way.) Then pin the other side, overlapping the straight edge with the scalloped edge to cover where there is no seam allowance. You'll detect a slight pucker at the base. This will be eliminated when you stitch. Start stitching where you have clipped. Fig. 24a.

Complete all the blocks. Complete the borders, leaving unstitched those areas indicated at each corner. They'll be finished after the top is assembled. The borders are intentionally designed not to be symmetrical and not to have repeats. That means you will experience less frustration and have less need to concentrate. You will be able to enjoy the stitching.

"Now we know the Campbell secrets for beautiful appliqué," agreed the Jacobean Four —
a name they had started calling themselves.

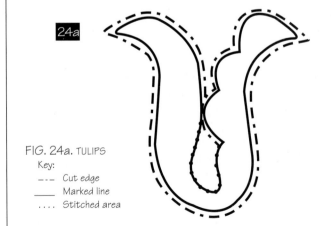

FIG. 24a. TULIPS
Key:
–·– Cut edge
___ Marked line
.... Stitched area

Let's see yours," pleaded Nina, as the Jacobean Four gathered
with their completed tops.
"You first," smiled Kate.
"We'll lay them out on the floor and look at them all together," suggested Mary.
"Ah, beautiful!" they sighed in unison.

CHAPTER V— ACROSS THE FINISH LINE

SEWING BLOCKS TOGETHER

■ Lay your blocks out for assembling. You can follow Fig. 25 or arrange them to suit yourself.

25

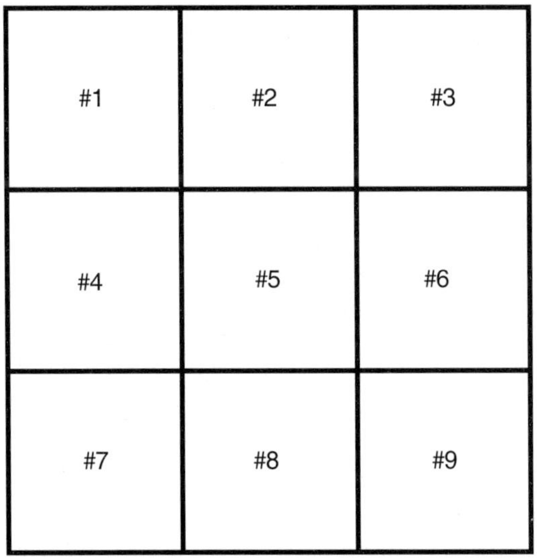

#1	#2	#3
#4	#5	#6
#7	#8	#9

FIG. 25. LAYOUT FOR SEWING BLOCKS TOGETHER

■ Turn the block over and fold it in half; then fold it in half the other way, making quarters. Mark lightly with a pencil the very center of the wrong side. Fig. 26. Do this for each of the nine blocks.

26

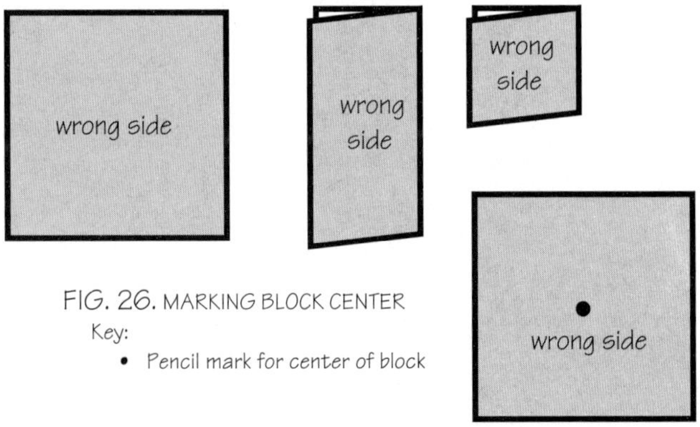

FIG. 26. MARKING BLOCK CENTER
Key:
• Pencil mark for center of block

■ Measure out from the marked center in all four directions 7.5". Fig. 27. With a T-square draw lines on all four sides for sewing.

27

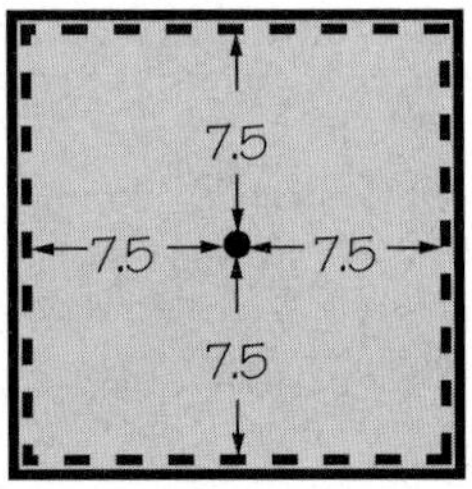

FIG. 27. MARKING SEWING LINE FOR 15" FINISHED BLOCK
Key:
• Center of block
– – – Sewing line

If you prefer, make a 15" square of cardboard or plastic. To find the center, draw diagonal lines. Fig. 28. Where the lines intersect, punch a small hole with the point of your scissors. Put a pin through the hole and into the pencil mark on your block. Square the template with your block, and then draw around the four sides with a pencil. These will be your sewing lines.

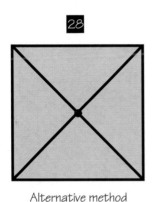

FIG. 28.
FINDING CENTER OF TEMPLATE SQUARE
Key:
* Center of block

■ Pin blocks #1, 2, and 3 together and sew along the marked lines. Do the same for #4, 5, 6 and for #7, 8, and 9.

■ Trim away the excess fabric, leaving a ¼" seam.

■ Press to one side or press open, as you prefer.

■ Pin and sew the three strips together, being careful that the blocks line up perfectly.

■ Trim the excess fabric, leaving ¼" seam. Press.

■ On the sewing line mark the center of each of the four sides.

■ Fold each border strip lengthwise, right side to right side, to find the center. On the wrong side make marks 5" from the fold on either side of it. Fig. 29. Do this at intervals that can be connected by pencil lines drawn to indicate the sewing line.

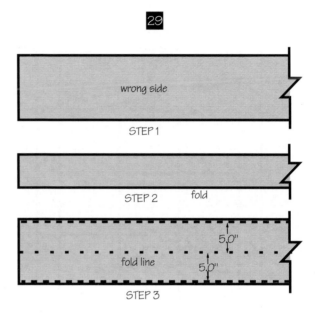

FIG. 29.
MARKING SEWING LINE FOR 10" FINISHED BORDER

SEWING ON BORDER STRIPS

■ Find the midpoint of the two shorter borders. Fig. 30. Pin, matching the center of the sewn blocks and the center of the border piece. Sew ¼" seams. Trim the excess. Press the seam.

■ Repeat for the two longer border strips. Find the midpoint, pin, stitch, and press. Fig. 30.

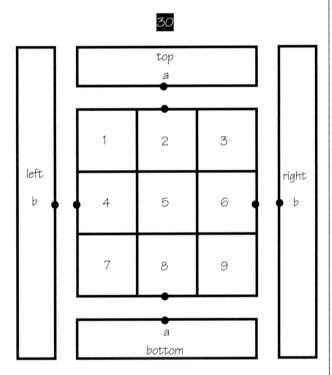

30

FIG. 30. LAYOUT FOR ASSEMBLING TOP

Key:
- • Midpoints for matching
- a Short border pieces
- b Long border pieces

■ Appliqué the corner pieces that were left unfinished.

■ Trim the outside edges of the assembled top to ¼" seam allowance.

QUILTING

Using your BF or another material, cut two pieces 69" long. Remove the selvages. Leave one length 44" wide (69" x 44"). From the other length, cut two widths 13" wide (69" x 13"). The back is made wider and longer than the front so that you can turn about 1½" on each side to the front while you are quilting. This protects the edge.

Sew the three lengths together, the wide one in the middle with the narrow pieces on each side. Fig. 31.

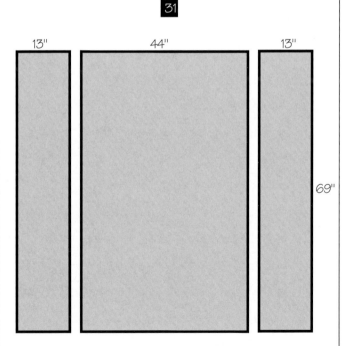

31

FIG. 31. LAYOUT FOR QUILT BACKING

Trim the two seams to ¼". Press open or to one side, as you prefer. Lay the backing on the floor or table, wrong side up.

Cut the batting 68" x 68". For a classical look try Hobbs Thermore®. If you prefer a higher loft, Hobbs Polydown® works well. Lay the batt on top of the backing. Then lay the quilt top, right side up, over the two. Baste the three layers together.

Quilting can be done in the open spaces and around the designs. Shadow quilting ⅛" to ¼" out from the designs makes the flowers and leaves puff. Stippling or meandering is pretty in the background and with the shadowing gives the whole top depth. In the quilt shown, the template patterns for the design pieces were used as quilting designs scattered randomly in the plain background spaces. Use quilting thread the color of your background, so your quilting design doesn't compete with the appliqué design.

When the quilting is completed, trim the excess batting and backing even with the quilt top.

ADDING A SLEEVE FOR HANGING

The sleeve can be made from any fabric — your leftover BF, one of your design fabrics, a contrasting plain colored fabric, even muslin.

■ Cut the piece 9" wide and 65" long. Fig. 32, Step 1.

■ Make double ¼" hems along each short end (turn under ¼" twice).

■ Measure 1½" from one of the long open edges. Fold along this line. Sew ½" with the basting stitch on your machine. Fig. 32, Step 2.

■ Fold the strip in half lengthwise with the open edges even. Fig. 32, Step 3.

■ Pin and sew the raw edges of the strip to the top of the quilt with ⅛" seam allowance. Notice it doesn't quite extend to each end. This is to permit you room to sew and turn the binding and still have the sleeve not show.

■ Pin and sew the lower edge of the sleeve by hand, using big stitches.

■ After you've sewn on the binding, remove the basting stitches. Liz Porter points out that this method permits extra easement to go over the rod, so that when the quilt is hung, the quilt doesn't curl forward and the sleeve doesn't show.

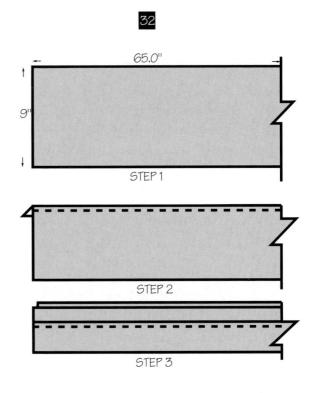

FIG. 32. PREPARATION OF SLEEVE

ADDING BINDING

You have cut two strips of binding. Sew the strips together. Gently finger press the seam. Ironing may cause stretching, which may cause the binding to wave.

Sew the binding to the quilt top:

■ Lay the binding, right side to ride side, on the quilt top, keeping the edges even. Start sewing about 4" from a corner, leaving a 2" binding tail unsewn. Fig. 33. Sew carefully, maintaining an even ¼" seam.

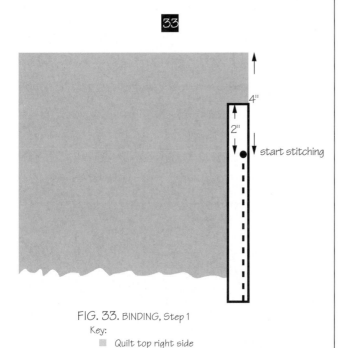

FIG. 33. BINDING, Step 1
Key:
▨ Quilt top right side
● Start sewing

■ Stop stitching ¼" from the corner. Backstitch. Clip thread. Fig. 34.

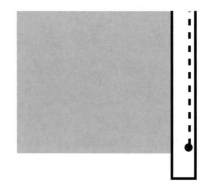

FIG. 34. BINDING, Step 2
Key:
▨ Quilt top right side
● Stop sewing

■ Fold the binding back on the diagonal, making a mitered corner. Fig. 35.

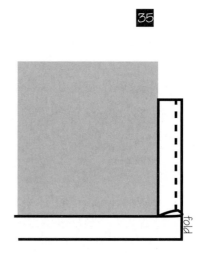

FIG. 35. BINDING, Step 3
Key:
▨ Quilt top right side

■ Turn the quilt.

■ Starting at the upper edge, sew a ¼" seam allowance to within ¼" of the next corner. Fig. 36.

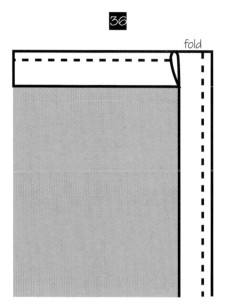

FIG. 36. BINDING, Step 4
Key:
▒ Quilt top right side

■ Repeat the above instructions at each corner.

■ About 2" from the end, stop sewing. Cut off the remaining binding, leaving a tail of 3". Fig. 37.

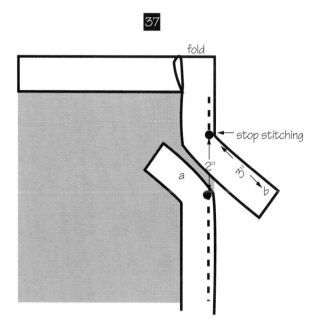

FIG. 37. BINDING, Step 5
Key:
▒ Quilt top right side
a piece left at beginning
b piece left at end

■ Fold the bottom piece (a) back diagonally. Fig. 38.

FIG. 38. BINDING, Step 6
Key:
▒ Quilt top right side
a piece left at beginning
b piece left at end

■ Hold and stitch the end piece (b) to meet the first sewing. Fig. 39.

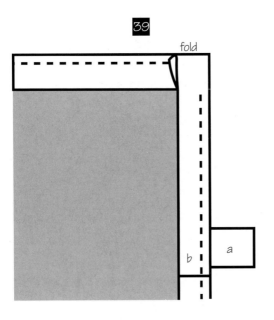

FIG. 39. BINDING, Step 7
Key:
▦ Quilt top right side
a piece left at beginning
b piece left at end

■ Trim the excess fabric.

■ Turn the binding to the wrong side, fold under ¼", pin, and stitch, using your newly-learned hidden appliqué technique. The stitches can be ¼" apart rather than the ¹⁄₁₆" you used on the design pieces. When you come to the corner, tack the miters down well, front and back. Push the needle back to the stitching line and continue stitching. At the point where the binding joins, trim the excess, and stitch the front and back with your hidden stitch.

DOCUMENTING YOUR QUILT

Make a label for the back, indicating the quilt name "Exotica," your name, the date, and any other information you think future generations may like to know. If you iron freezer paper on the back of your label before writing on it, you'll find you can write with ease. A Sharpie® pen has permanent ink and is easy to use to write on fabric. A Pigma® pen, which comes in a range of colors, can be used to decorate the label with your logo or with Jacobean flowers. Sew the label into the lower corner of your quilt, after you've removed the paper.

Store your templates in a plastic envelope.

Take a photograph for your scrapbook.

Show "Exotica" with pride. You have created a family heirloom.

At a guild meeting the Jacobean Four showed their completed "Exotica" quilts.
When the members "oo'd" and "ah'd" over them, Nina announced, "We're going to write to Pat and Mimi to find out if they're doing another book with new designs. We'll let you know!"

EXOTICA

PATTERN & COLOR PLATE SECTION

EXOTICA - BLOCK #1
Stitched by Grace Sohn, Essex, Connecticut

Numbers indicate templates and letters indicate stitching order.

BLOCK #1
Upper Left Quadrant

13

15

15R

14

16

17

5

Center line

5

4

3

2

2R

*Start Here

10

11

Center line

BLOCK #1
Lower Left Quadrant

44

6

8

9

1

BLOCK #1
Lower Right Quadrant

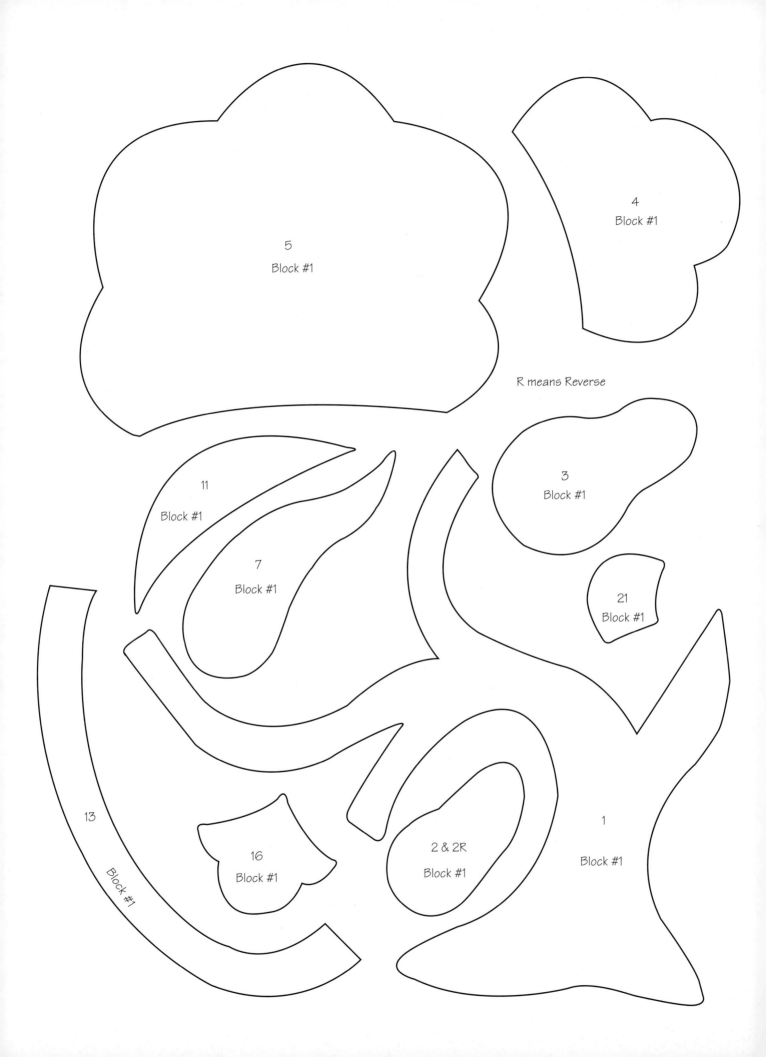

5
Block #1

4
Block #1

R means Reverse

11
Block #1

3
Block #1

7
Block #1

21
Block #1

13

Block #1

16
Block #1

2 & 2R
Block #1

1

Block #1

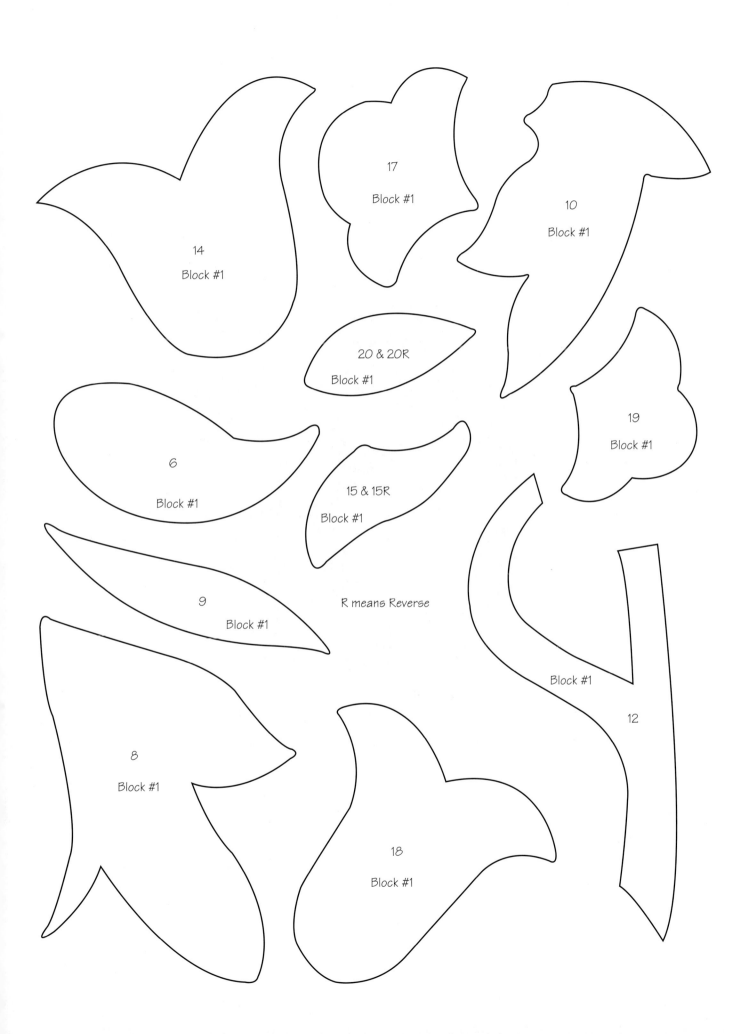

EXOTICA - BLOCK #2
Stitched by Roslyn Hay, Australia

Center
line

Center
line

Center
line

Center
line

BLOCK #2
Upper Left Quadrant

Center
line

6

5

1

Center
line

BLOCK #2
Lower Left Quadrant

52

3

1

BLOCK #2
Lower Right Quadrant

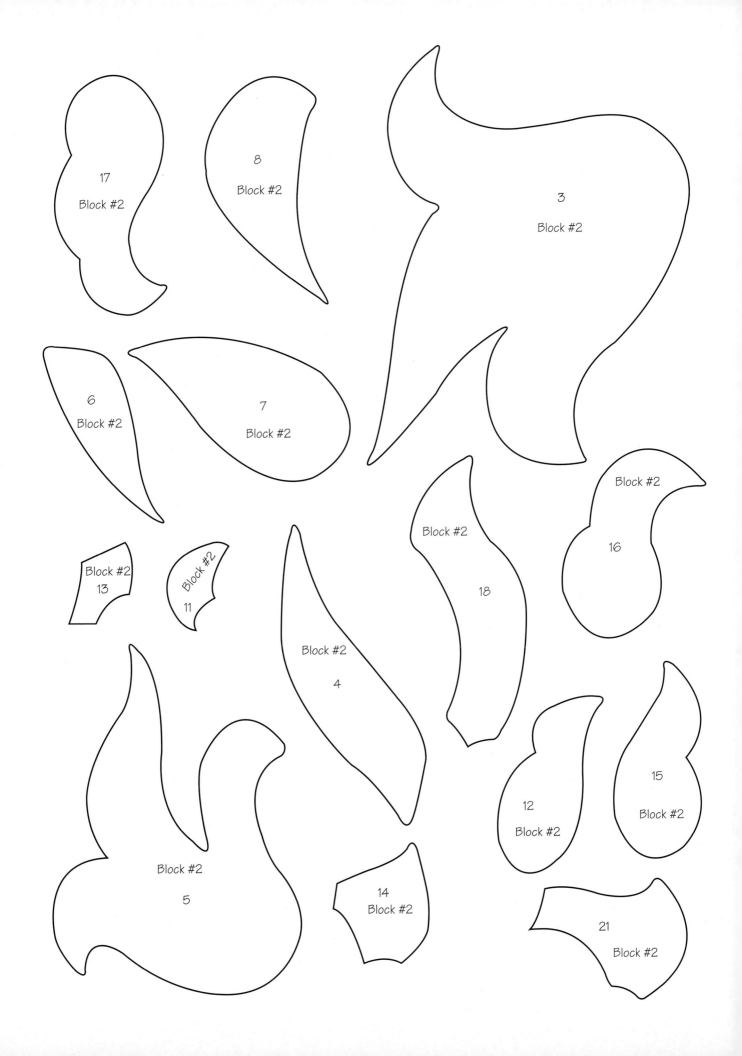

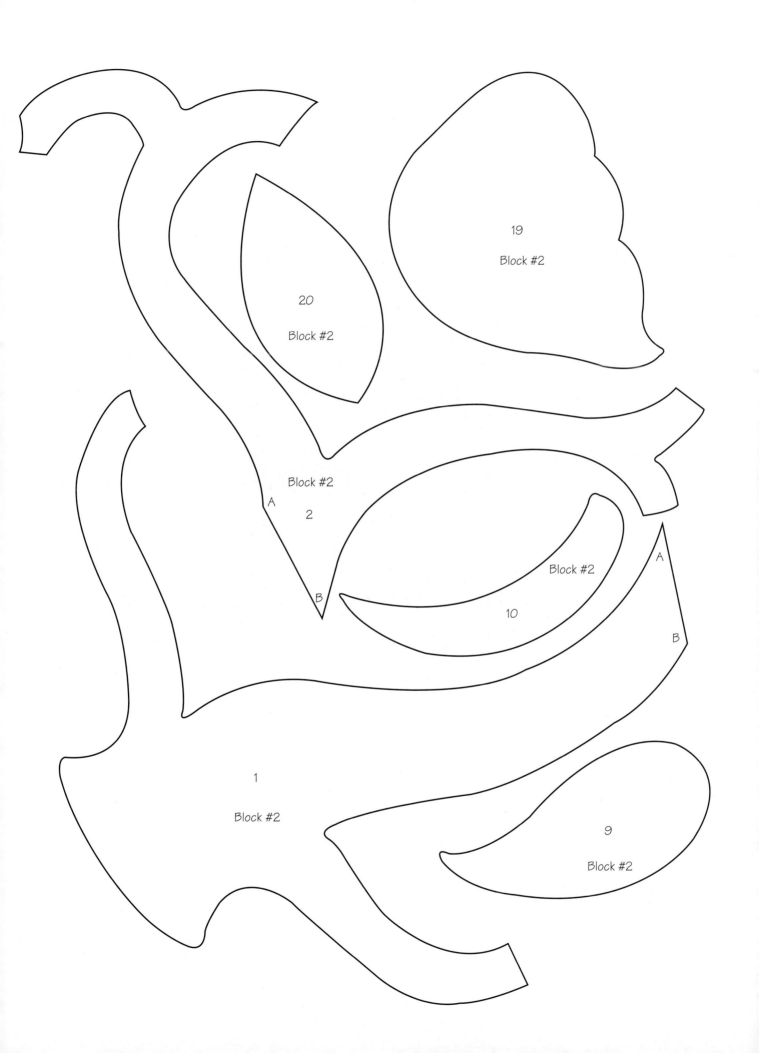

EXOTICA - BLOCK #3
Stitched by Michelle Jack, Garland, Texas

BLOCK #3
Upper Left Quadrant

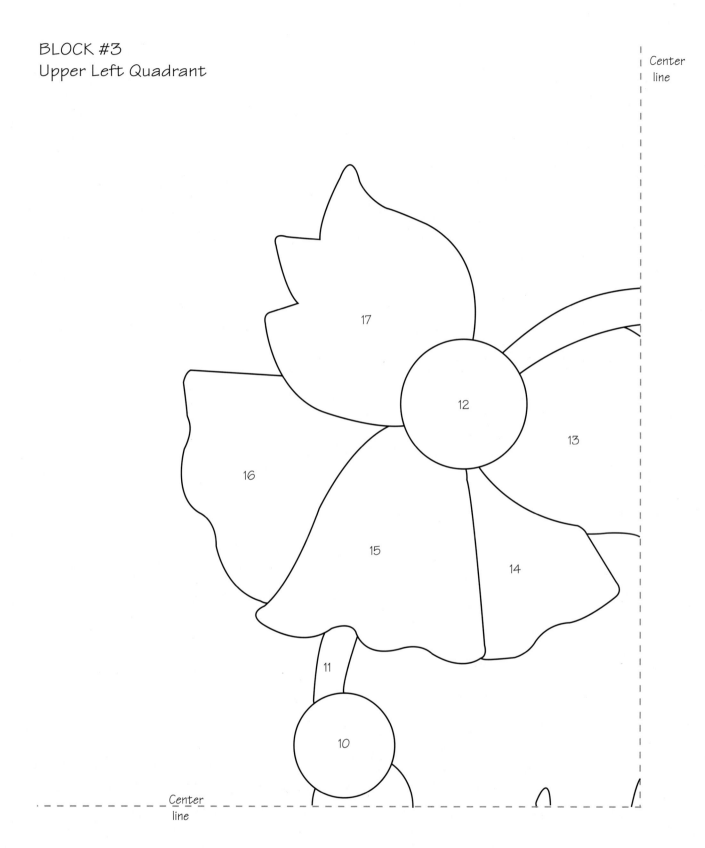

Center line

17

12

13

16

15

14

11

10

Center line

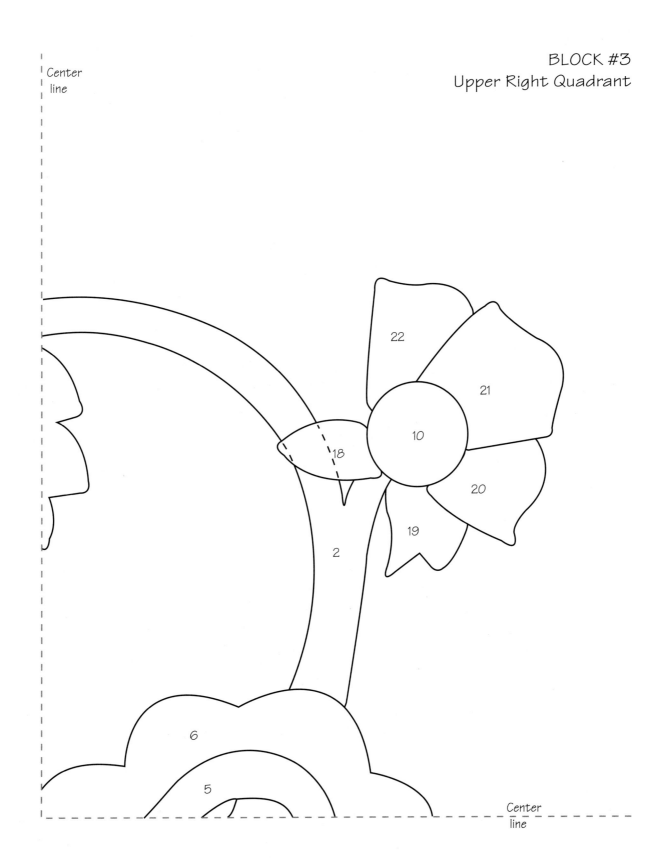

Center
line

22

21

10

18

20

19

2

6

5

Center
line

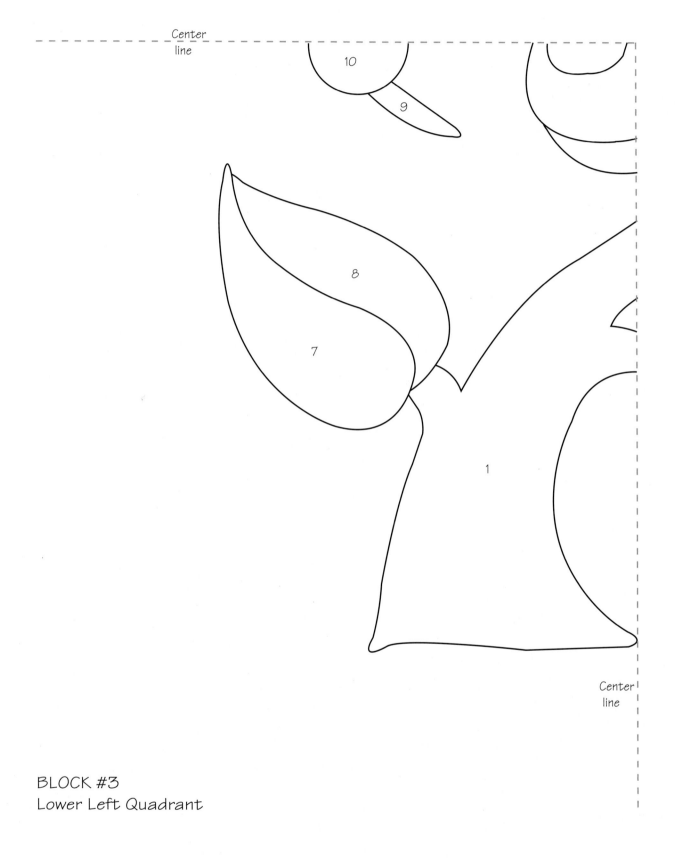

10

9

8

7

1

BLOCK #3
Lower Left Quadrant

Center
line

Center
line

4

3

BLOCK #3
Lower Right Quadrant

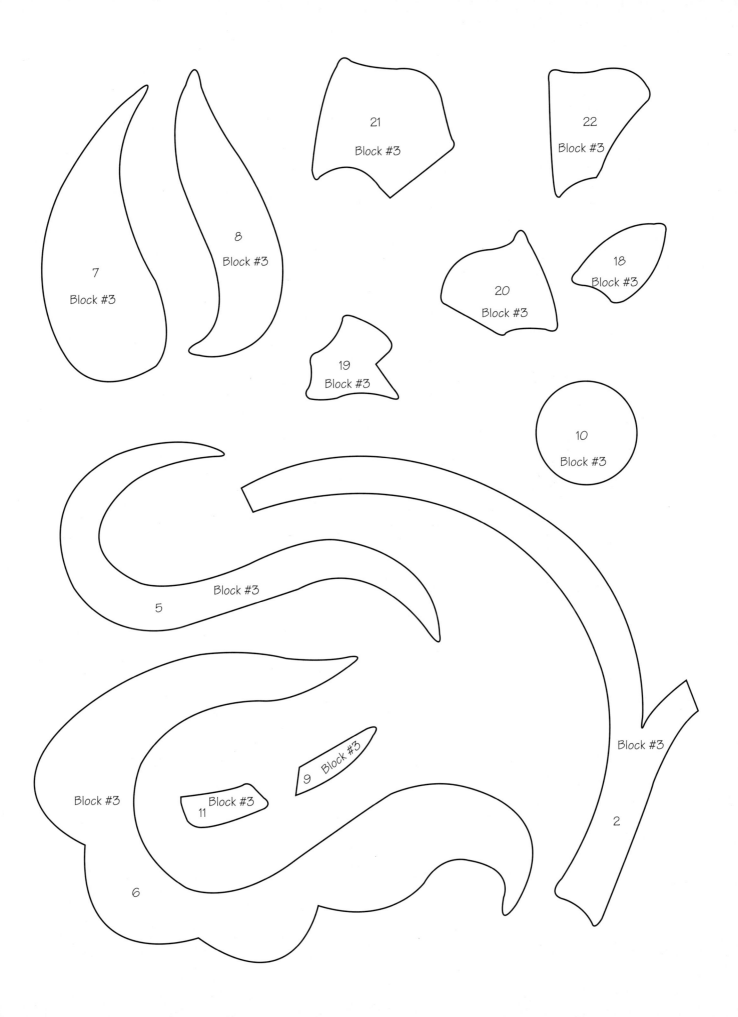

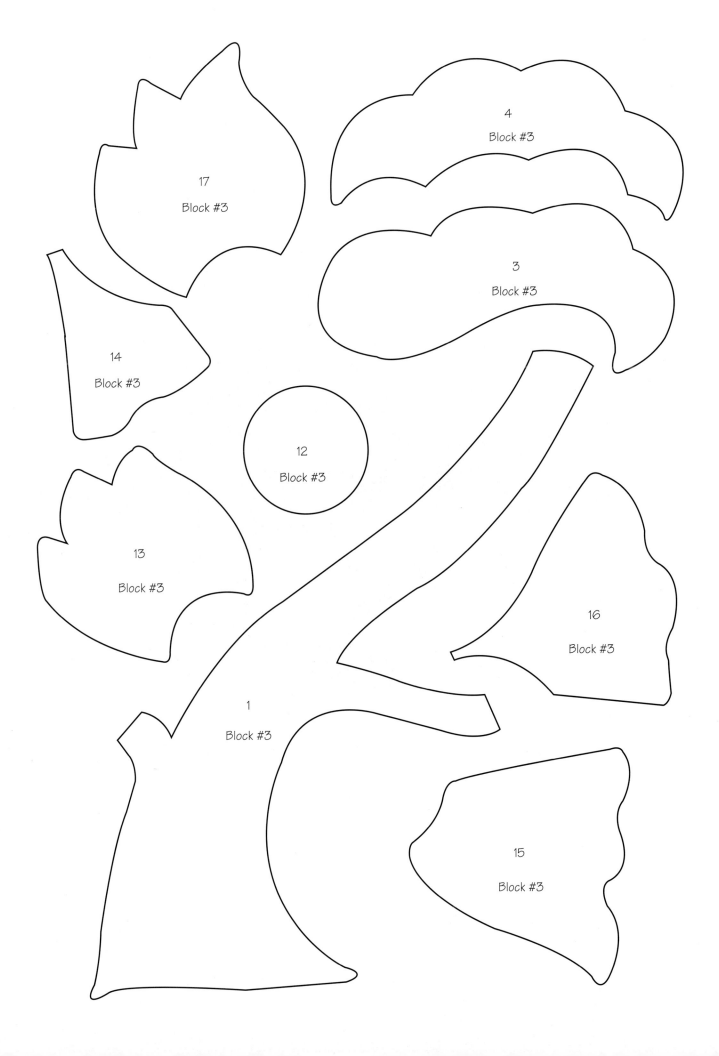

17
Block #3

4
Block #3

3
Block #3

14
Block #3

12
Block #3

13
Block #3

16
Block #3

1
Block #3

15
Block #3

EXOTICA - BLOCK #4
Stitched by Sharon Chambers, Mesquite, Texas

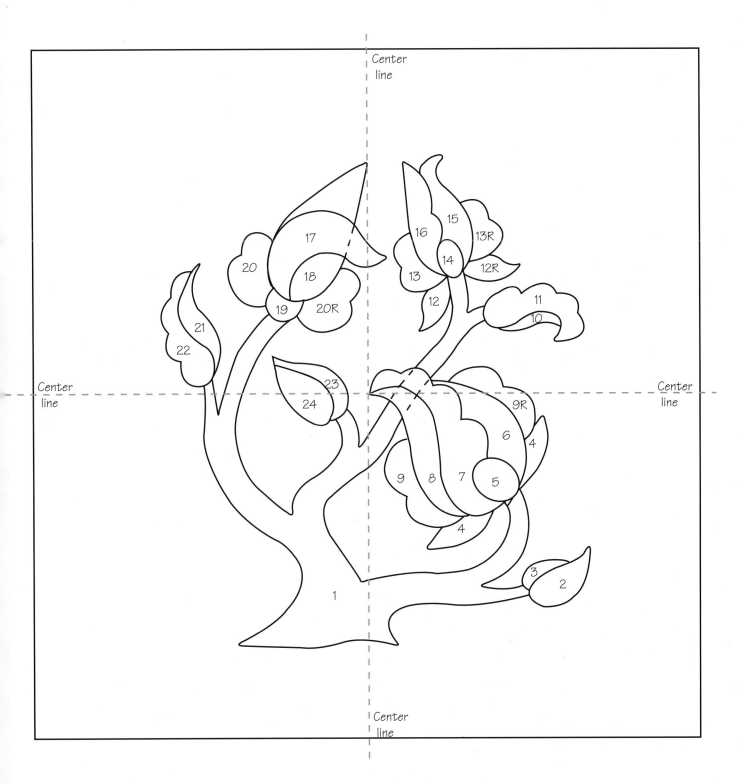

BLOCK #4
Upper Left Quadrant

Center
line

17

20

18

20R

19

21

22

23

Center
line

Center
line

Center
line

67

Center
line

24

1

Center
line

BLOCK #4
Lower Left Quadrant

9R

6

4

9

8

7

5

4

3

2

BLOCK #4
Lower Right Quadrant

69

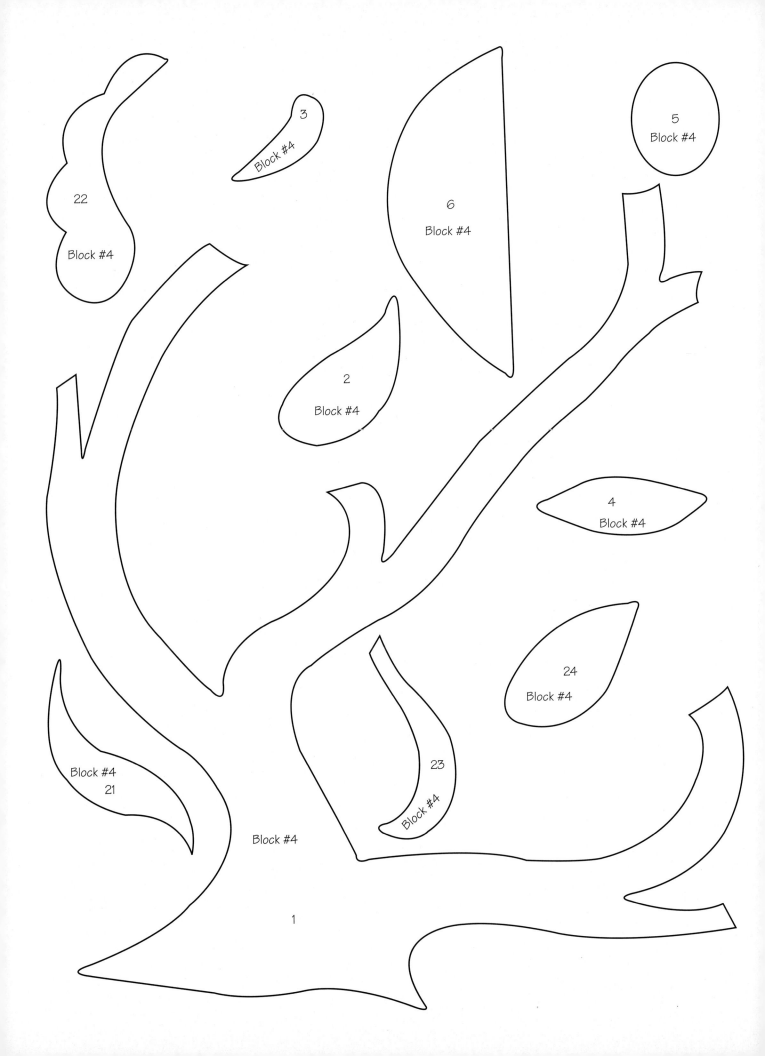

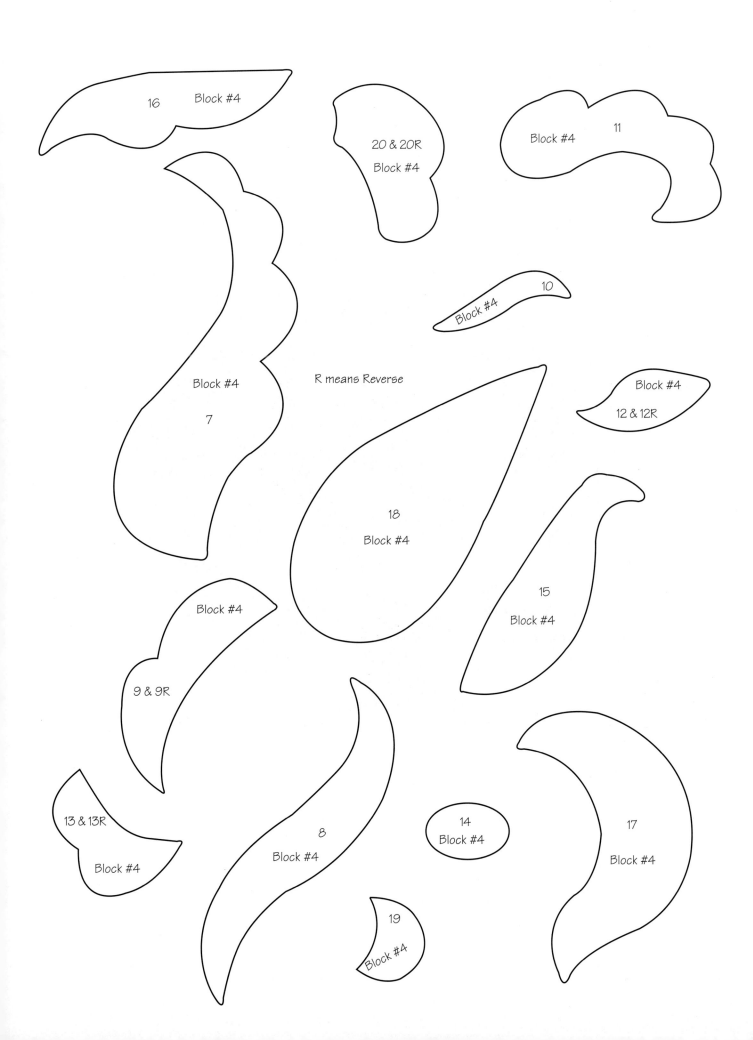

16   Block #4

20 & 20R
Block #4

Block #4   11

Block #4   10

R means Reverse

Block #4
12 & 12R

Block #4

7

18

Block #4

Block #4

15

Block #4

9 & 9R

13 & 13R

Block #4

8

Block #4

14
Block #4

17

Block #4

19

Block #4

EXOTICA - BLOCK #5
Stitched by Maureen A. Carlson, Moline, Illinois

BLOCK #5
Upper Left Quadrant

8R

9

3

6R

6R

6

6R

6R

6R

6

3

Center
line

7

3R

2

5

4

6

6

6

6

6R

6R

6R

6R

A

B

6R

6

6

6

6

6

6

10

11

9

9

1

BLOCK #5
Lower Left Quadrant

9

8

7

9

5

4

BLOCK #5
Lower Right Quadrant

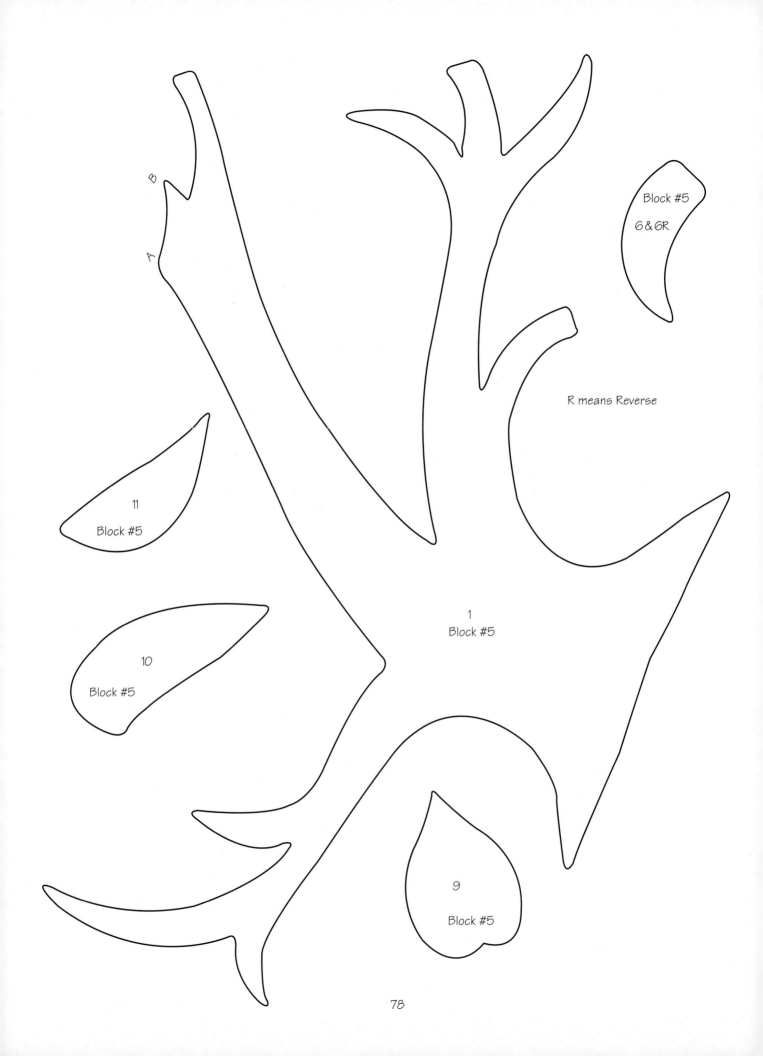

B

A

Block #5
6 & 6R

R means Reverse

11

Block #5

1

Block #5

10

Block #5

9

Block #5

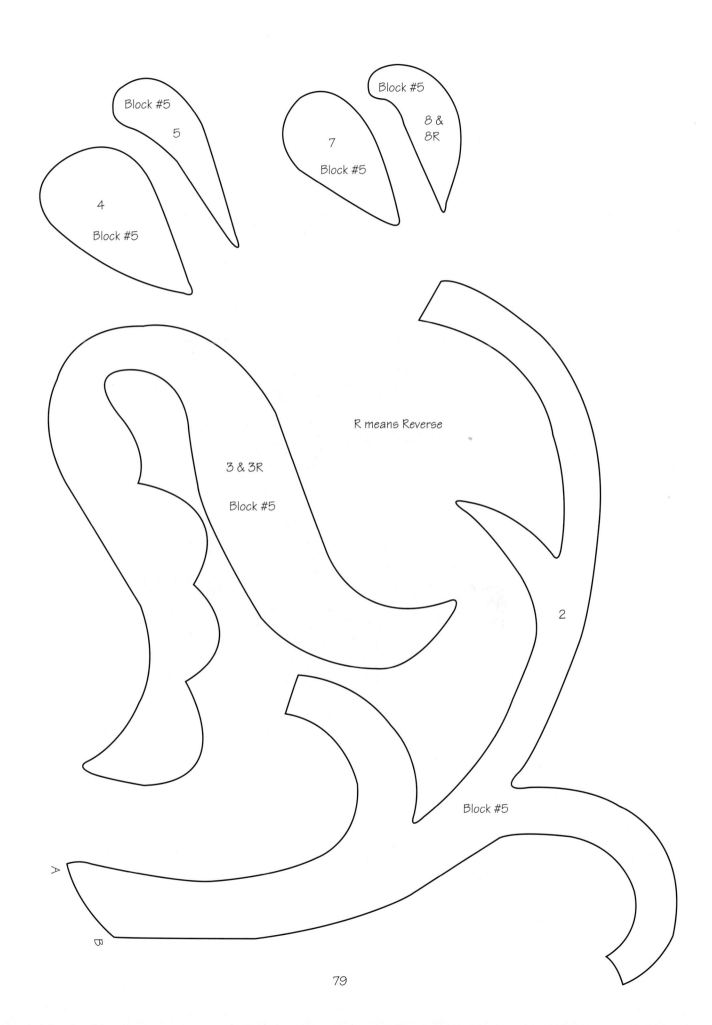

Block #5

5

Block #5

7

Block #5

Block #5

8 &
8R

4

Block #5

R means Reverse

3 & 3R

Block #5

2

Block #5

A

B

79

EXOTICA - BLOCK #6
Stitched by Jennifer Patriarche, Redmond, Washington

BLOCK #6
Upper Left Quadrant

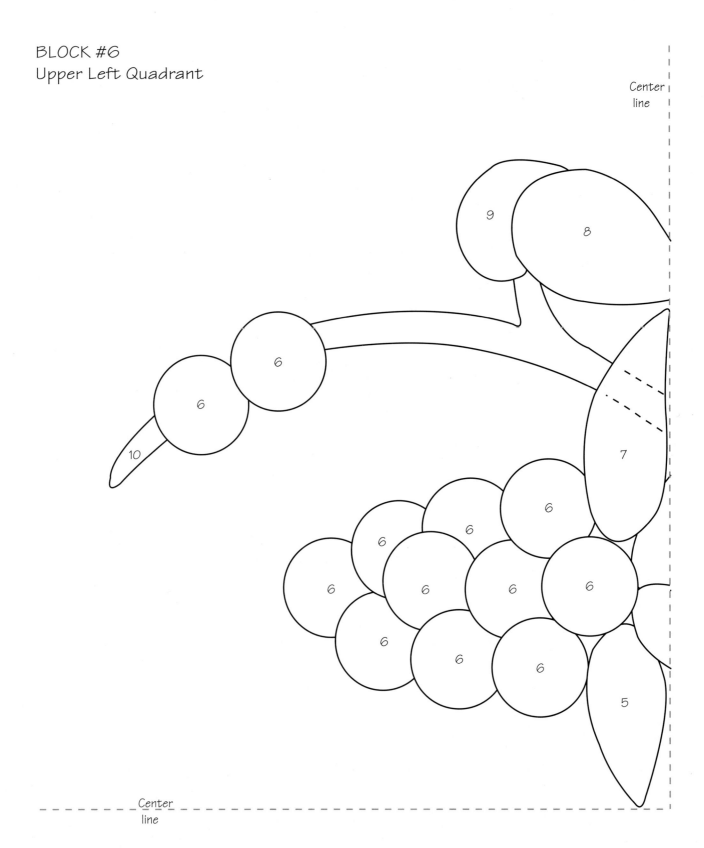

82

Center
line

Center
line

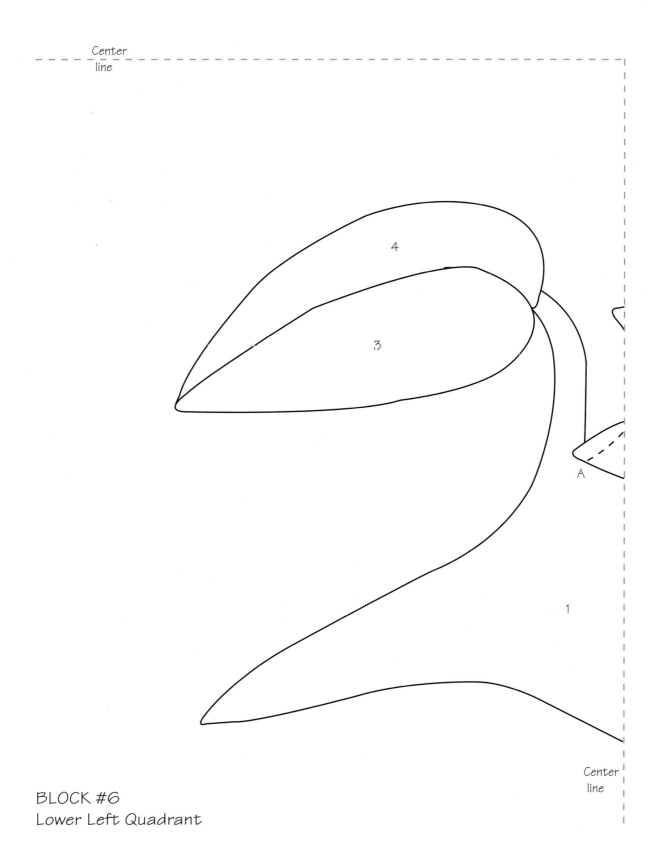

4

3

A

1

BLOCK #6
Lower Left Quadrant

Center
line

Center
line

BLOCK #6
Lower Right Quadrant

85

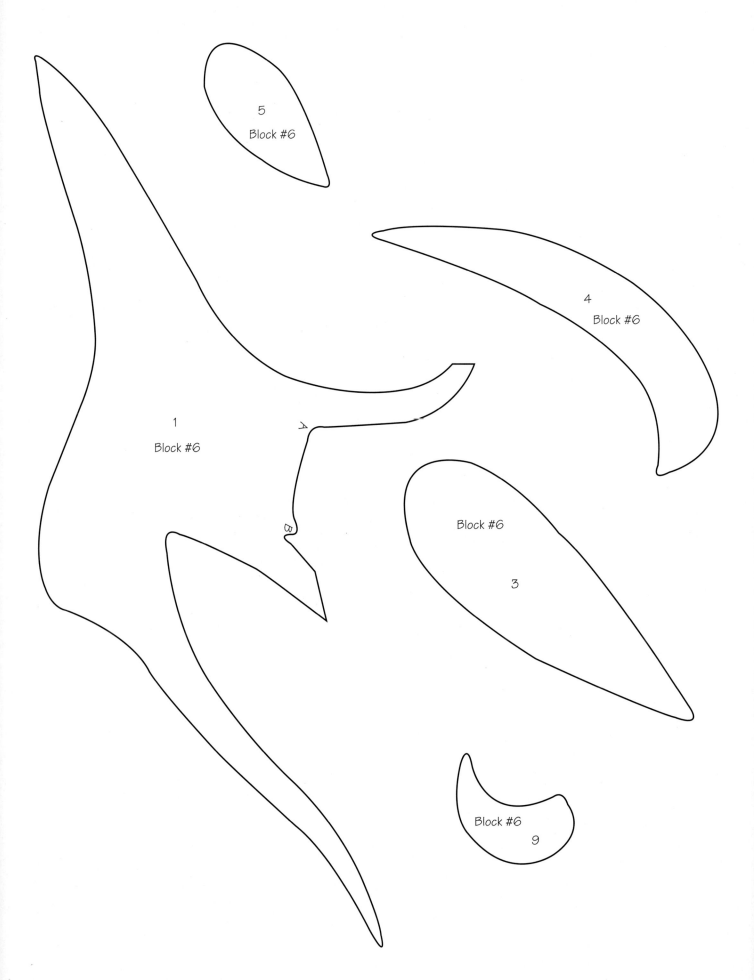

5
Block #6

4
Block #6

1
Block #6

A

B

Block #6

3

Block #6

9

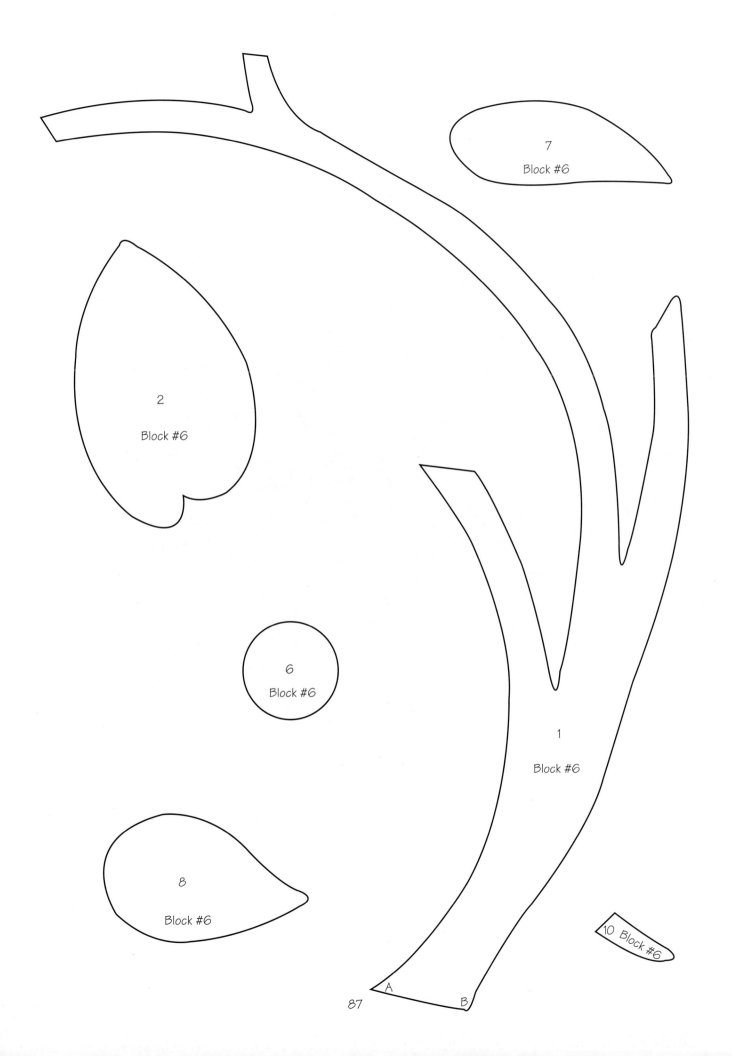

7
Block #6

2
Block #6

6
Block #6

1
Block #6

8
Block #6

10   Block #6

A
B

87

EXOTICA - BLOCK #7
Stitched by Nancy J. Steidle, Santa Fe, New Mexico

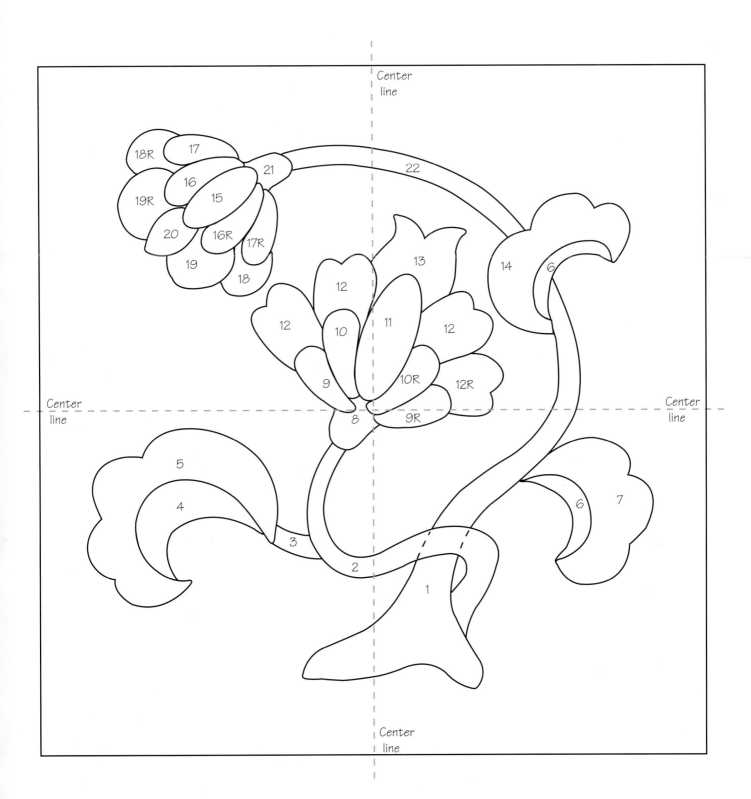

BLOCK #7
Upper Left Quadrant

18R

17

21

16

19R

15

20

16R

17R

19

18

12

12

10

9

Center
line

22

13

14

6

11

12

10R

12R

8

5

4

3

2

BLOCK #7
Lower Left Quadrant

Center
line

9R

6

7

1

Center
line

BLOCK #7
Lower Right Quadrant

2

14

Block #7

Block #7

20

Block #7

4

Block #7

6

Block #7

7

Block #7

12& 12R

Block #7

13

Block #7

11

Block #7

R means Reverse

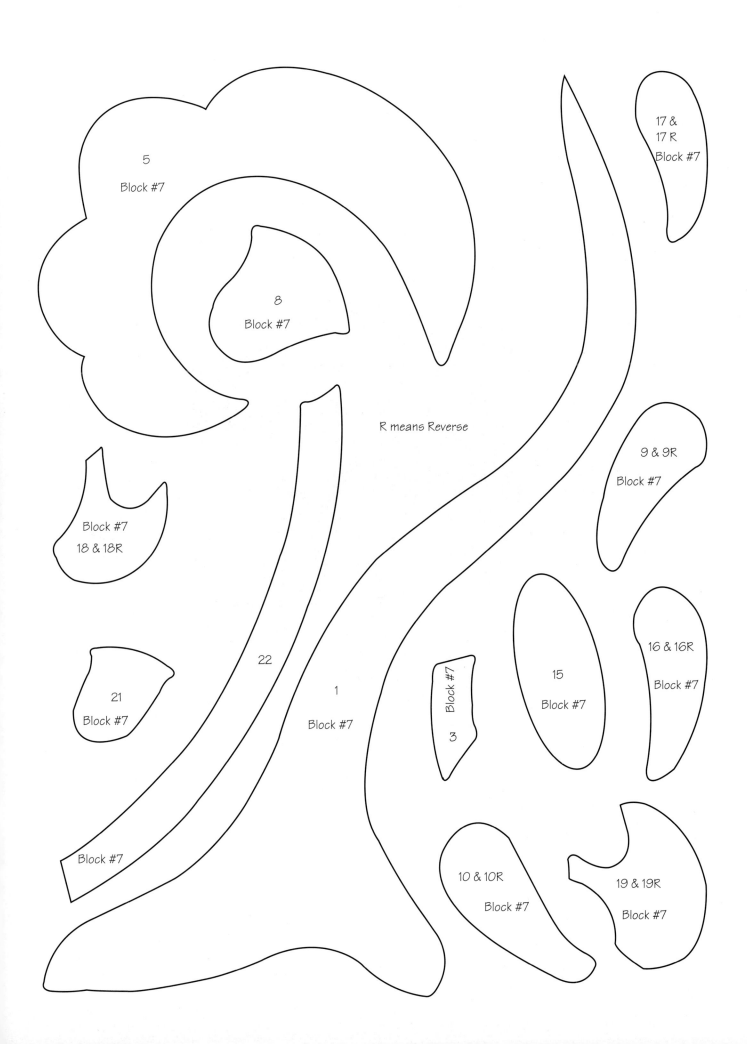

EXOTICA - BLOCK #8
Stitched by Gail Kessler, Oley, Pennsylvania

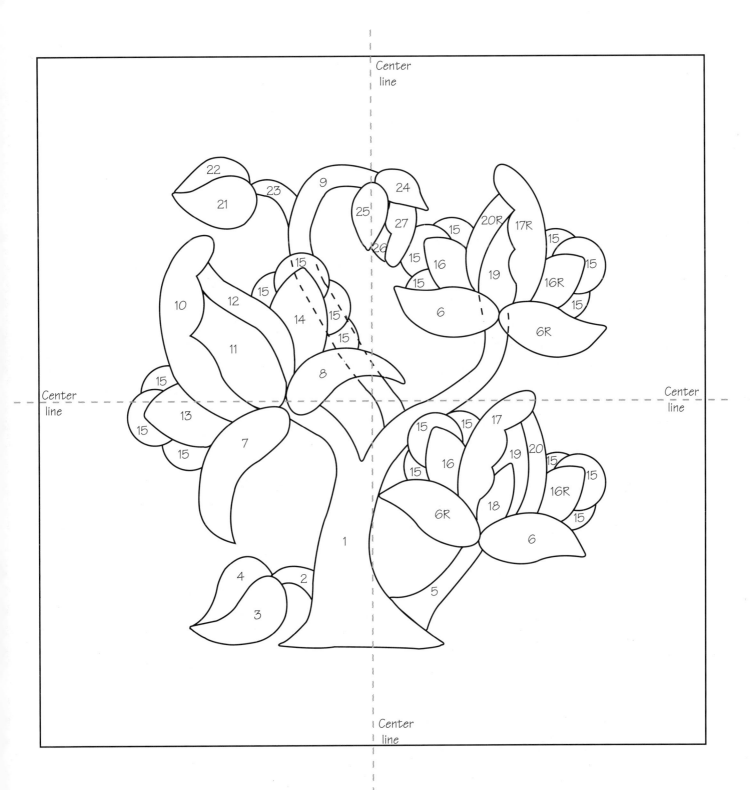

BLOCK #8
Upper Left Quadrant

Center line

Center
line

Center
line

24

27

26

20R

15

17R

15

15

15

16

19

16R

15

15

6

6R

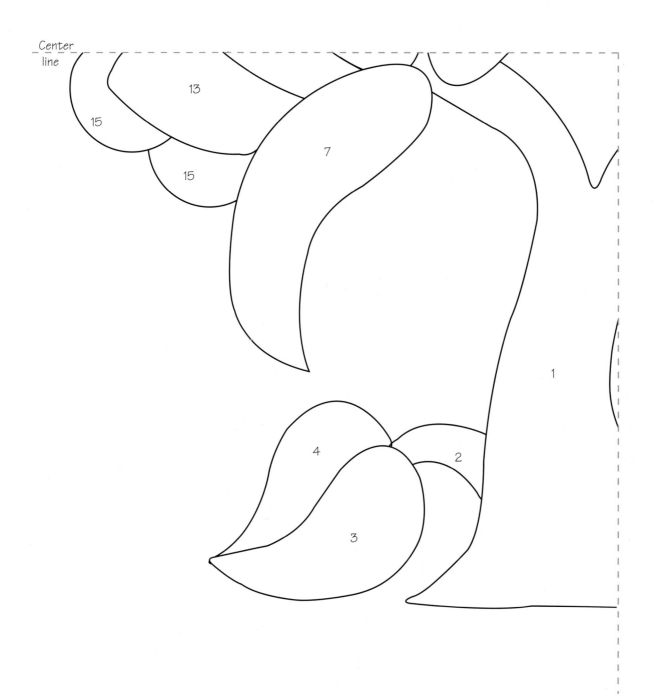

BLOCK #8
Lower Left Quadrant

15

15

17

16

15

19

20

15

15

15

16R

18

6R

15

6

5

BLOCK #8
Lower Right Quadrant

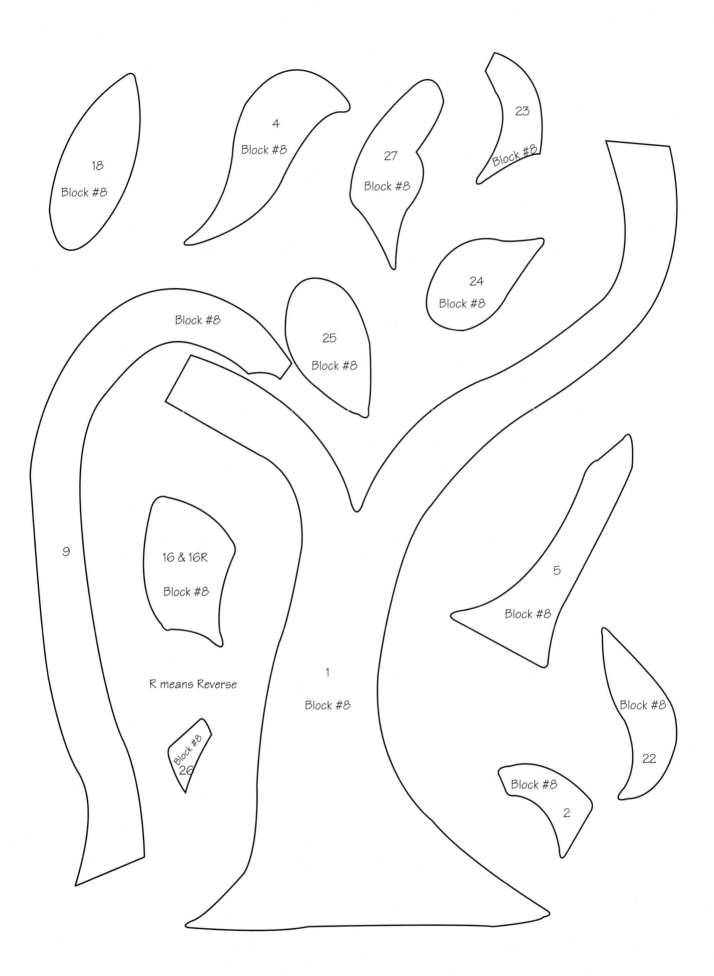

18

Block #8

4

Block #8

27

Block #8

23

Block #8

24

Block #8

Block #8

25

Block #8

9

16 & 16R

Block #8

R means Reverse

Block #8

26

5

Block #8

Block #8

22

1

Block #8

Block #8

2

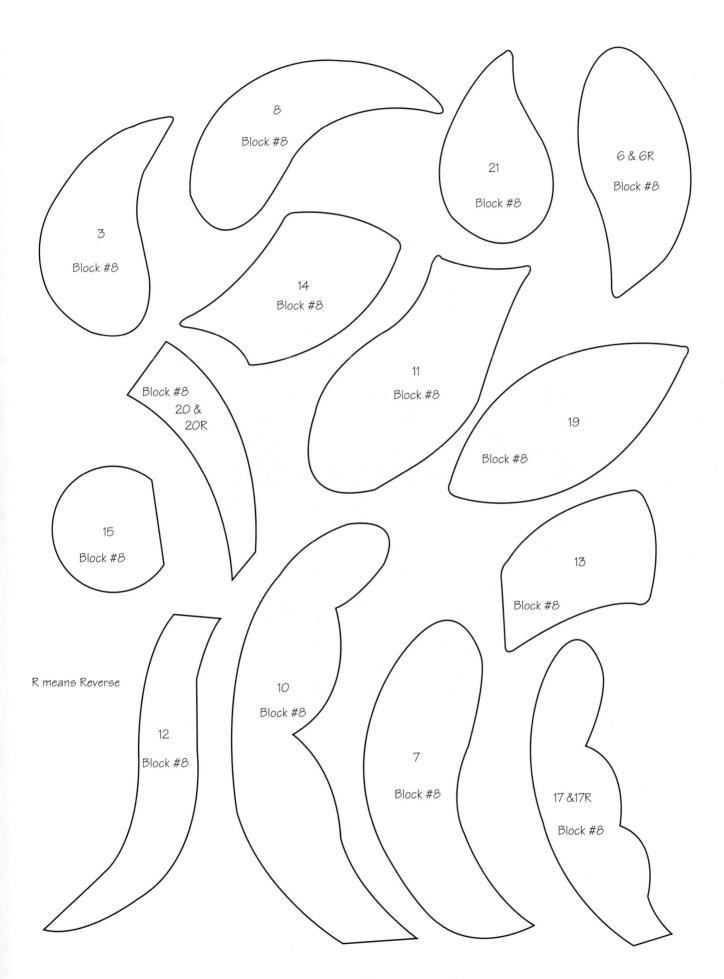

8

Block #8

21

Block #8

6 & 6R

Block #8

3

Block #8

14

Block #8

Block #8
20 &
20R

11

Block #8

19

Block #8

15

Block #8

13

Block #8

R means Reverse

10

Block #8

12

Block #8

7

Block #8

17 &17R

Block #8

EXOTICA - BLOCK #9
Stitched by Sally Ashbacher, Rowlett, Texas

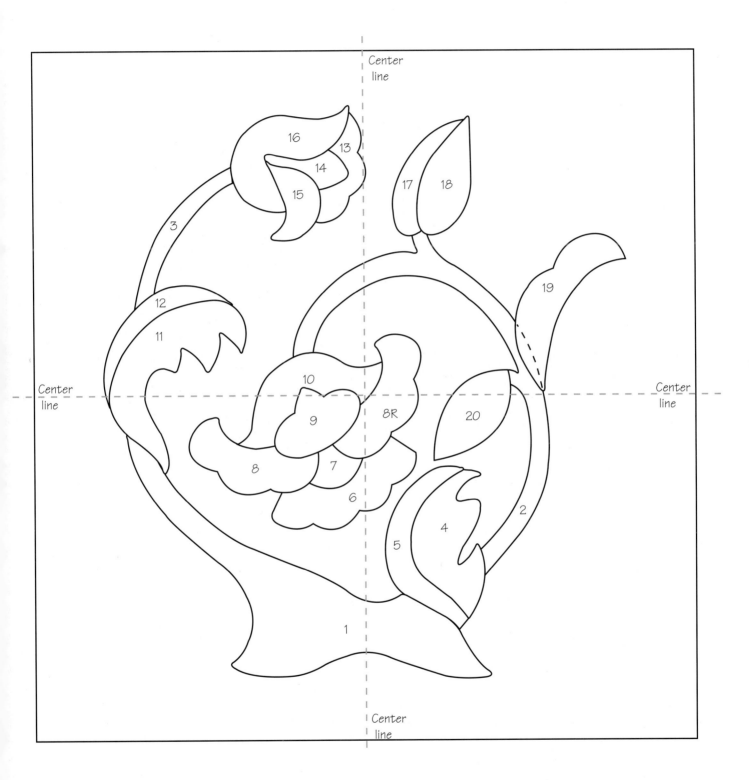

BLOCK #9
Upper Left Quadrant

16

13

14

15

3

12

11

Center
line

10

BLOCK #9
Upper Right Quadrant

17

18

19

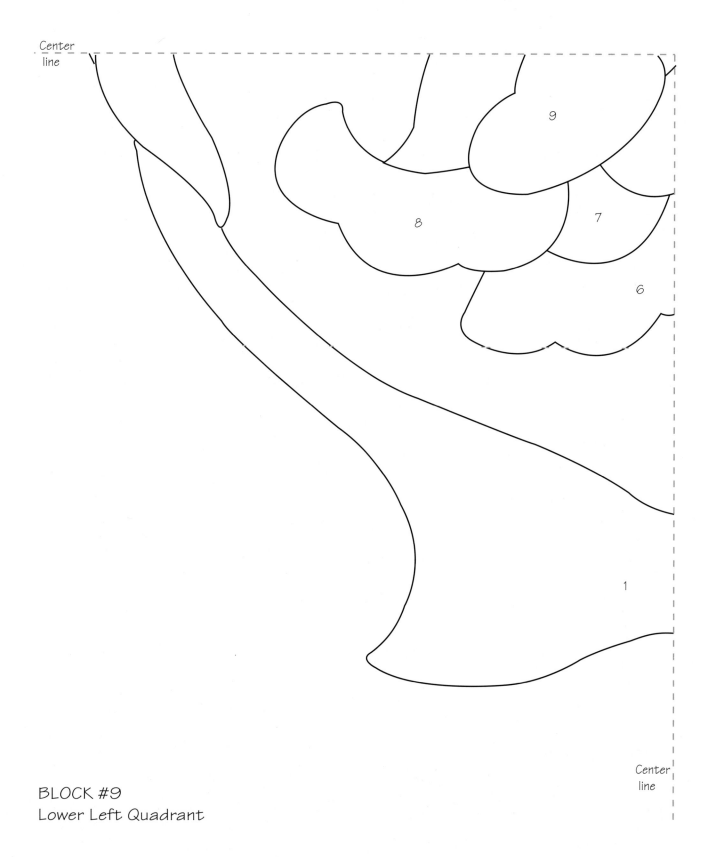

Center
line

Center
line

9

8

7

6

1

BLOCK #9
Lower Left Quadrant

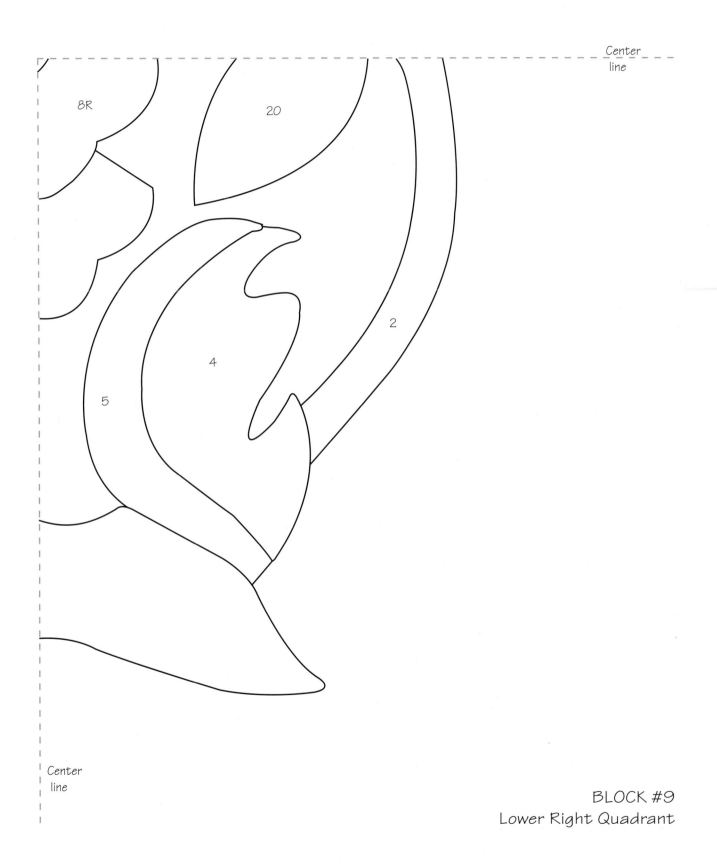

8R

20

2

4

5

BLOCK #9
Lower Right Quadrant

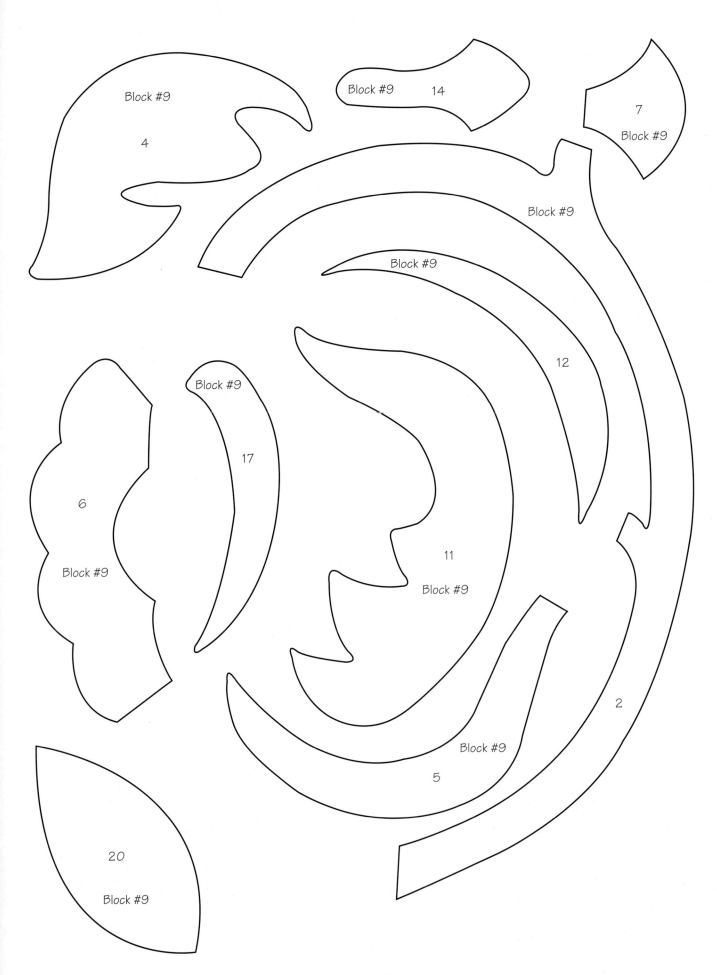

Block #9

4

Block #9   14

7

Block #9

Block #9

Block #9

Block #9

12

Block #9

17

6

11

Block #9

Block #9

2

Block #9

5

20

Block #9

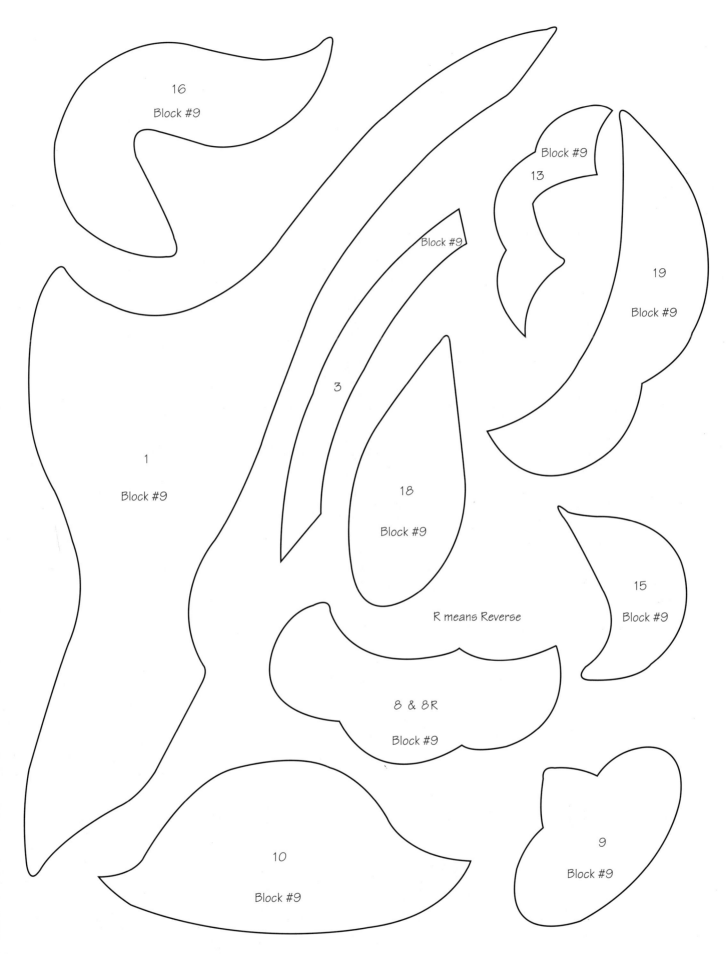

16
Block #9

Block #9
13

Block #9

19

Block #9

Block #9

3

1

Block #9

18

Block #9

R means Reverse

15
Block #9

8 & 8R

Block #9

10

Block #9

9

Block #9

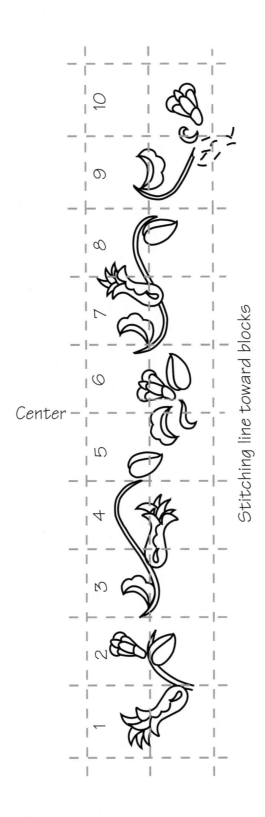

10   9   8   7   6   Center   5   4   3   2   1

Stitching line toward blocks

EXOTICA - LEFT BORDER

Stitched by Stephanie J. Braskey, Pottstown, Pennsylvania

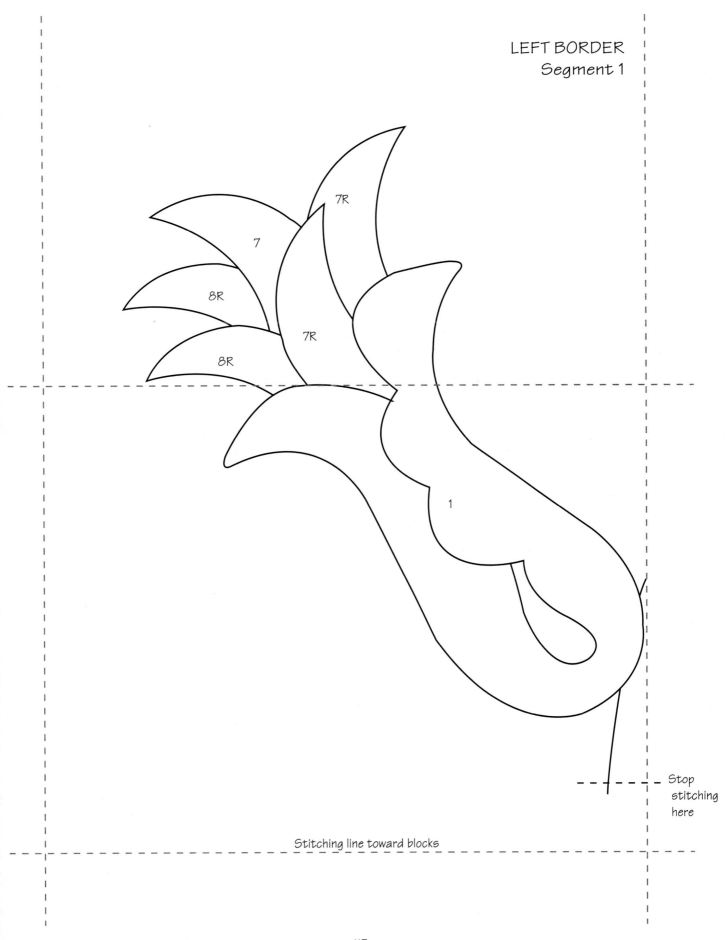

LEFT BORDER
Segment 1

7R

7

8R

7R

8R

1

Stop
stitching
here

Stitching line toward blocks

113

LEFT BORDER
Segment 2

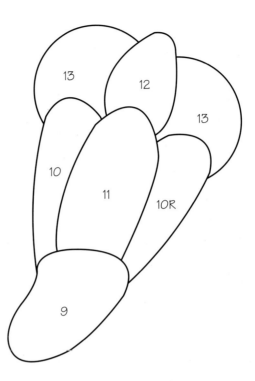

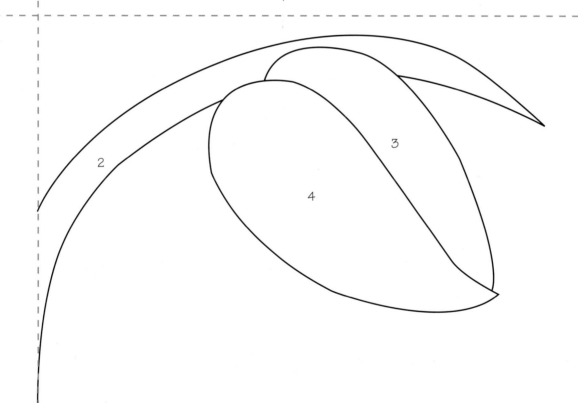

Stitching line toward blocks

6

5

Stitching line toward blocks

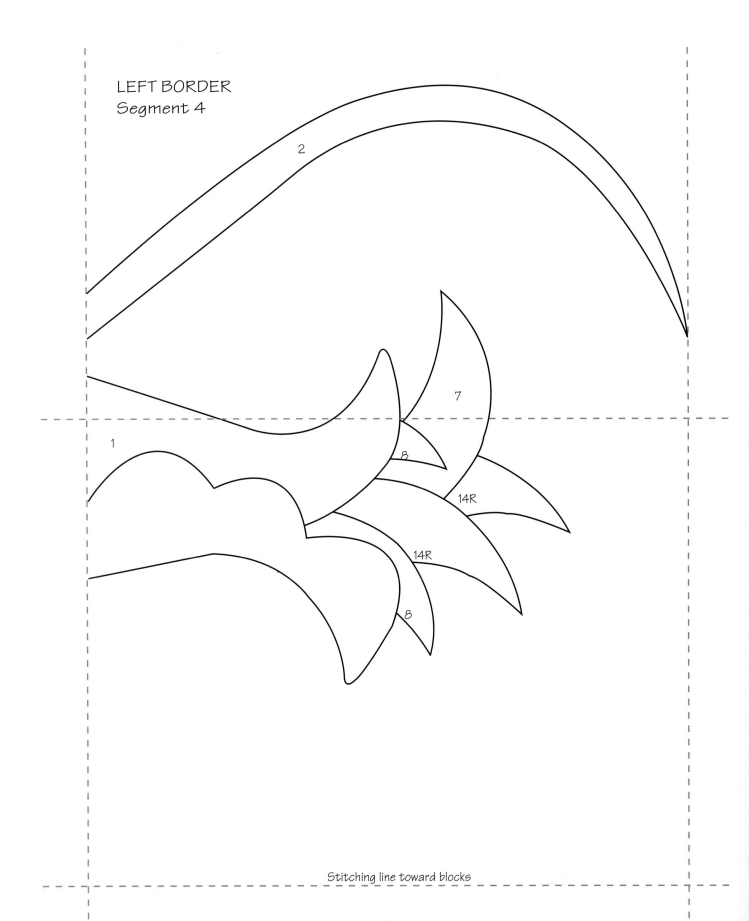

LEFT BORDER
Segment 4

2

7

1

8

14R

14R

8

Stitching line toward blocks

116

Center line

4

3

5

6

15

Stitching line toward blocks

Stitching line toward blocks

LEFT BORDER
Segment 7

14R

8R

14R

7R

6

5

Stitching line toward blocks

119

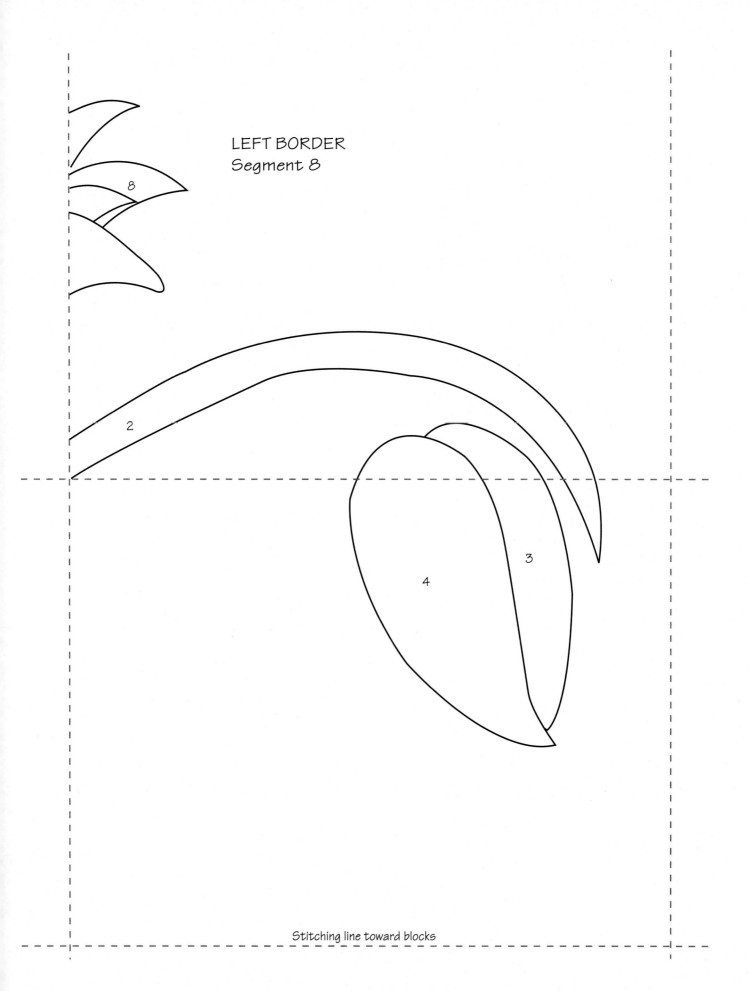

LEFT BORDER
Segment 8

8

2

4

3

Stitching line toward blocks

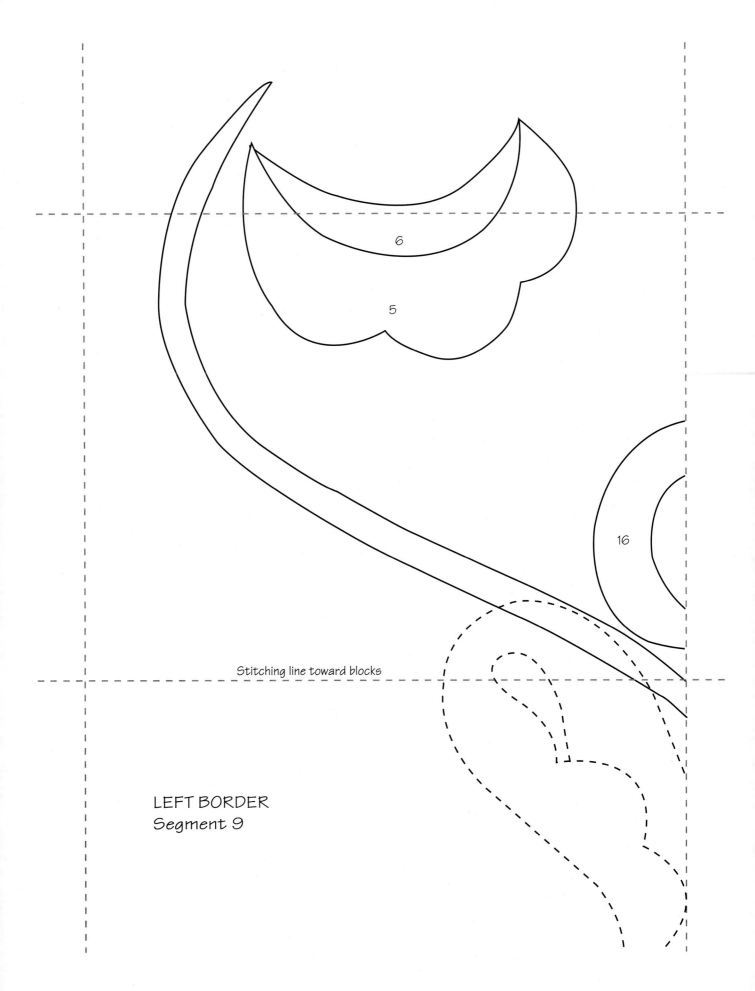

6

5

16

Stitching line toward blocks

LEFT BORDER
Segment 9

LEFT BORDER
Segment 10

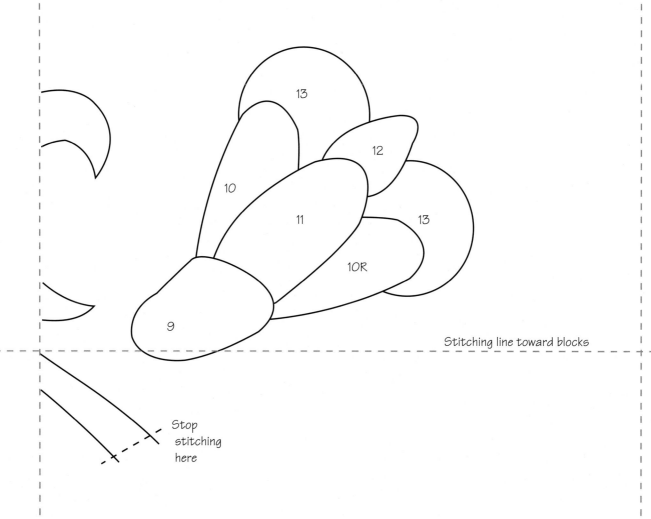

13

12

10

11

13

10R

9

Stitching line toward blocks

Stop
stitching
here

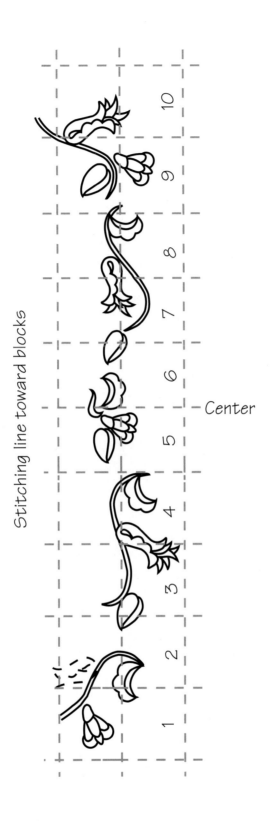

Stitching line toward blocks

Center

10 9 8 7 6 5 4 3 2 1

EXOTICA- RIGHT BORDER

Stitched by JoAnna Thomason Shampine, Richardson, Texas

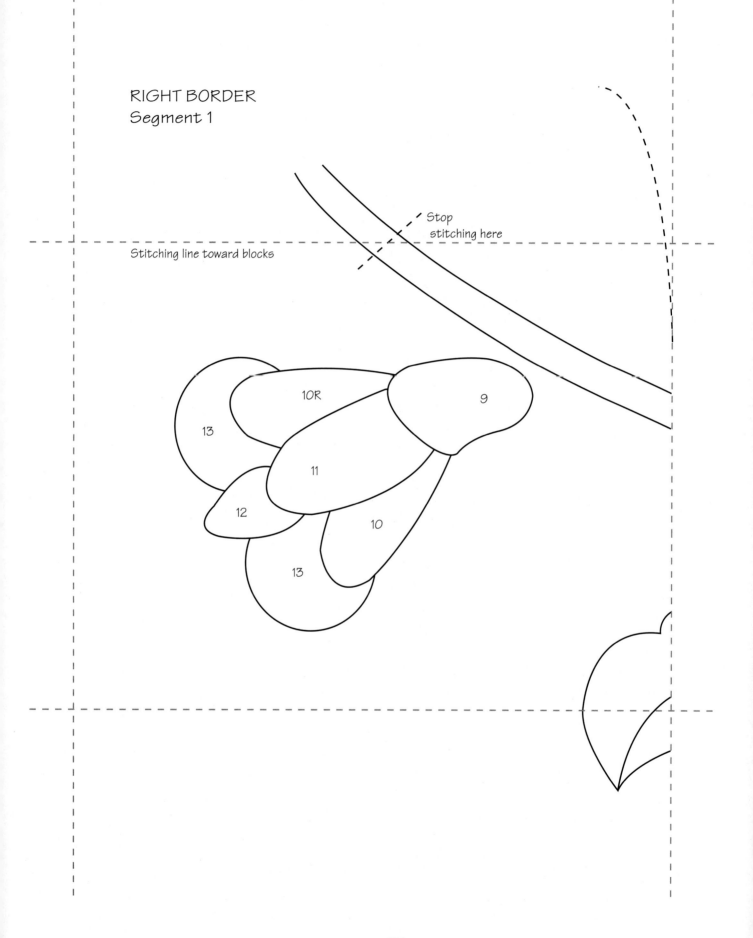

RIGHT BORDER
Segment 1

Stitching line toward blocks

Stop
stitching here

13

10R

9

11

12

10

13

RIGHT BORDER
Segment 2

Stitching line toward blocks

5

2

6

3

RIGHT BORDER
Segment 3

2

8

7R

14

7R

8R

RIGHT BORDER
Segment 4

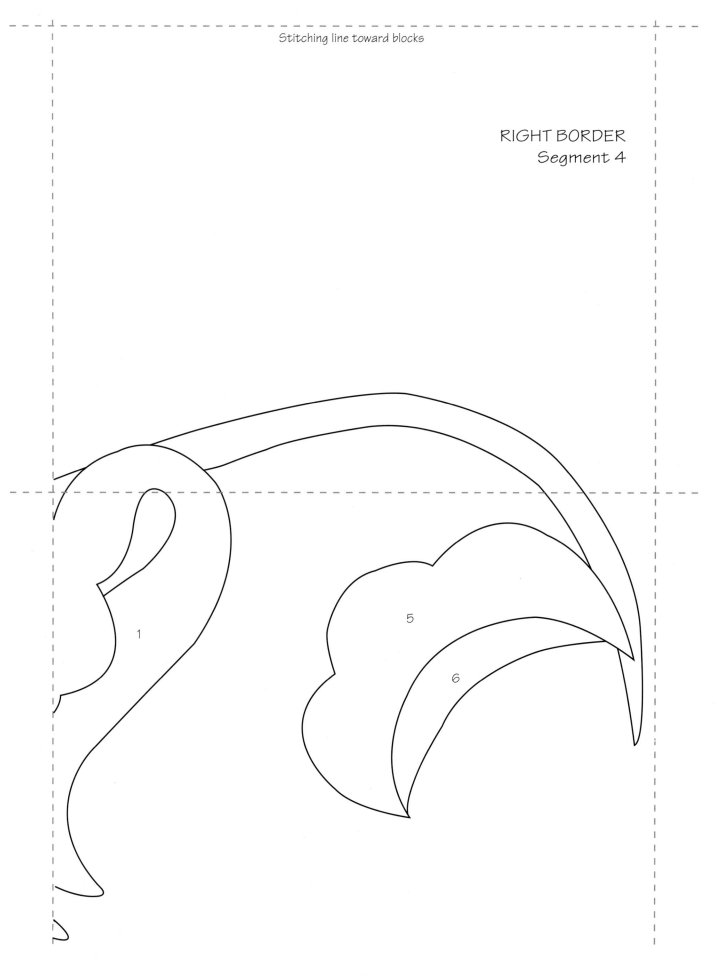

RIGHT BORDER
Segment 5

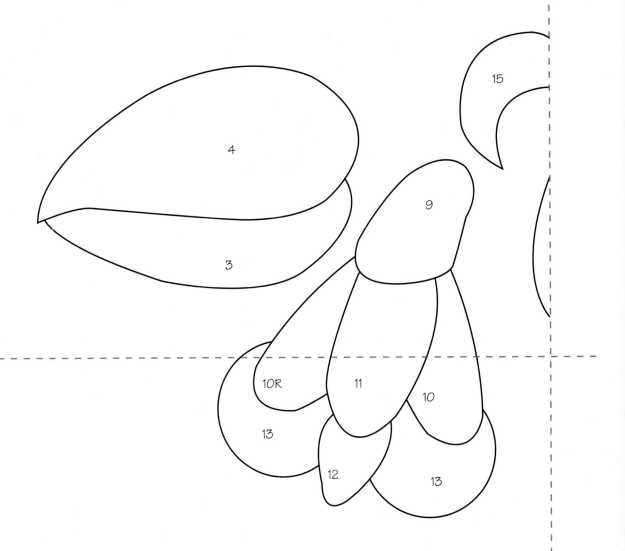

Center line

Stitching line toward blocks

6

5

4

3

RIGHT BORDER
Segment 7

8

7

14

8R

2

RIGHT BORDER
Segment 8

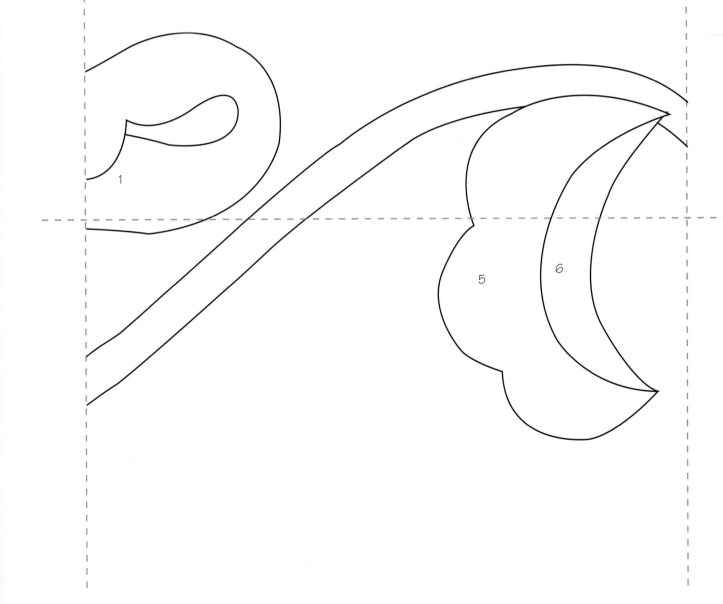

1

5

6

RIGHT BORDER
Segment 9

Stitching line toward blocks

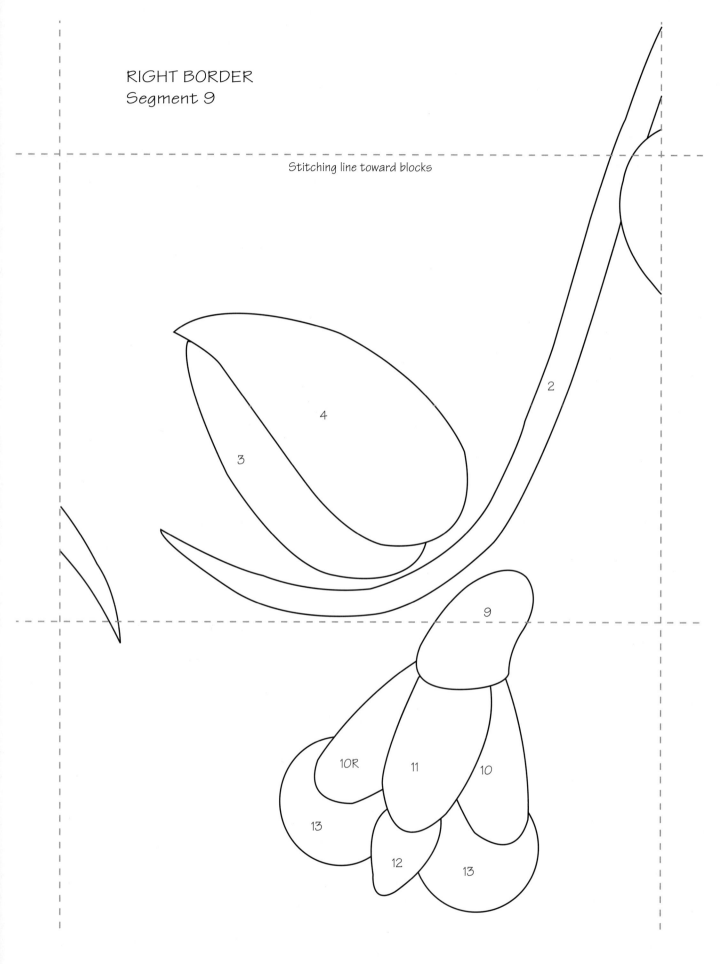

132

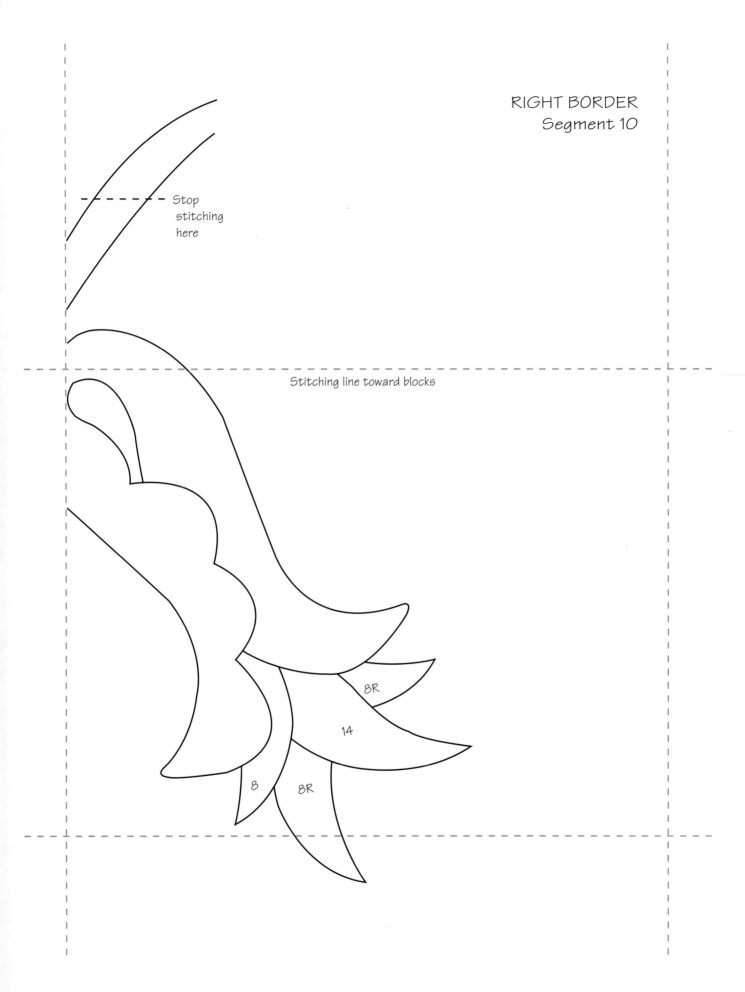

RIGHT BORDER
Segment 10

Stop
stitching
here

Stitching line toward blocks

8R

14

8

8R

Center

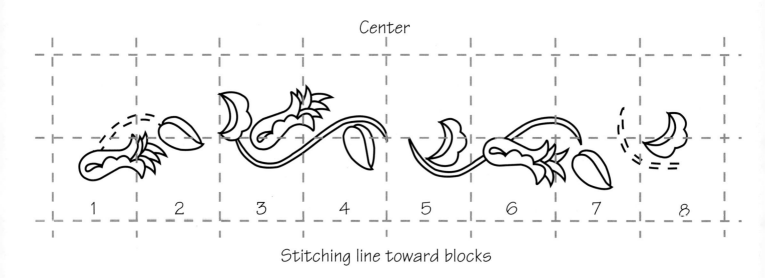

1   2   3   4   5   6   7   8

Stitching line toward blocks

EXOTICA- TOP BORDER
Stitched by Pat Campbell, Dallas, Texas

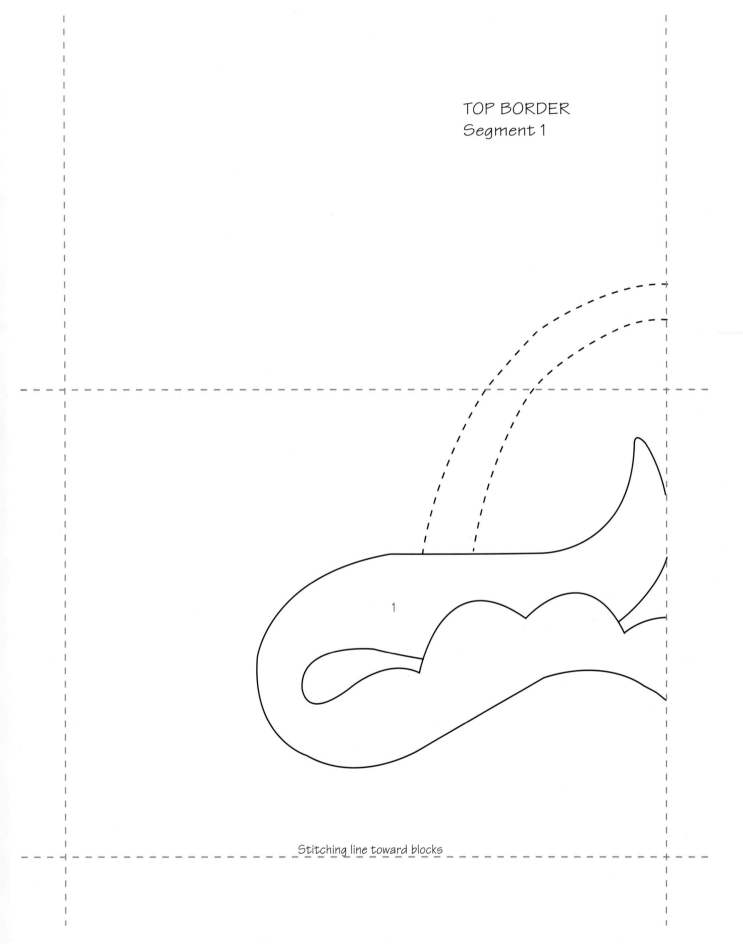

TOP BORDER
Segment 1

1

Stitching line toward blocks

TOP BORDER
Segment 2

3

4

14

8R

14R

14R

8

Stitching line toward blocks

136

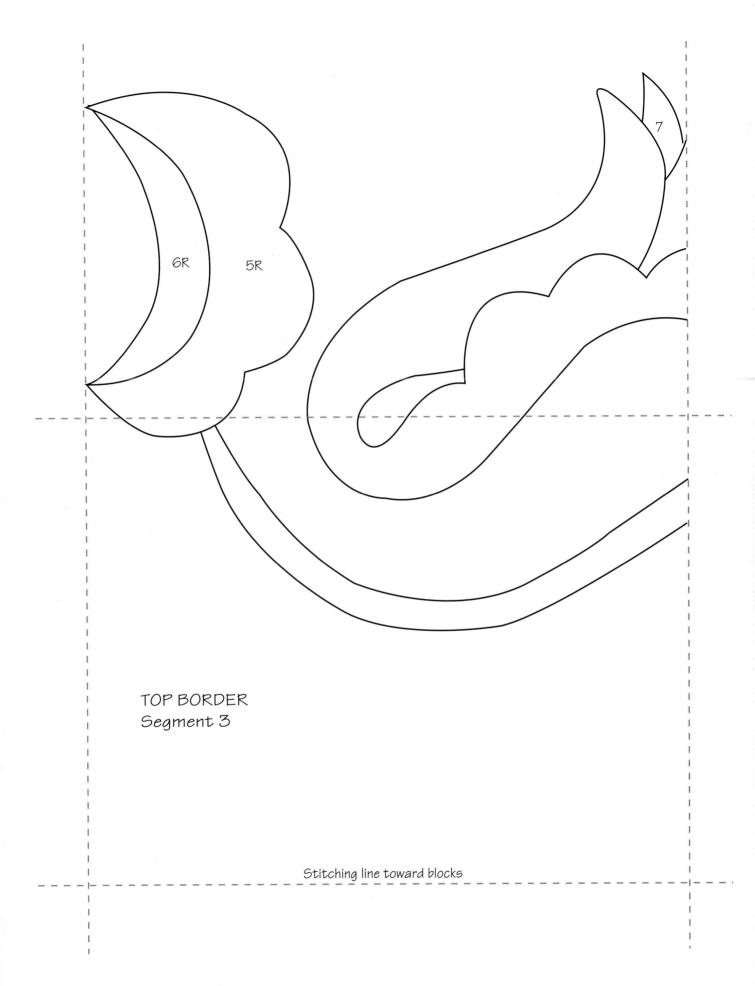

6R

5R

7

TOP BORDER
Segment 3

Stitching line toward blocks

TOP BORDER
Segment 4

8R

14R

8

8

2

4

3

Stitching line toward blocks

TOP BORDER
Segment 5

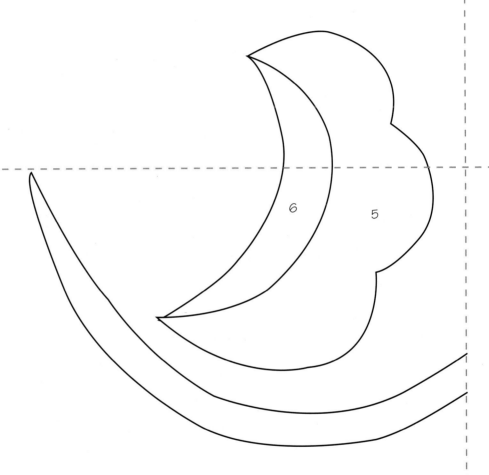

6

5

Stitching line toward blocks

TOP BORDER
Segment 6

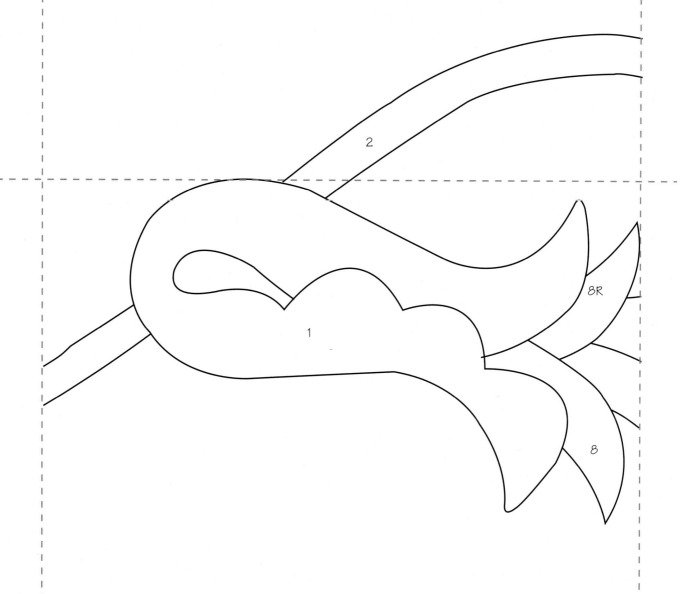

Stitching line toward blocks

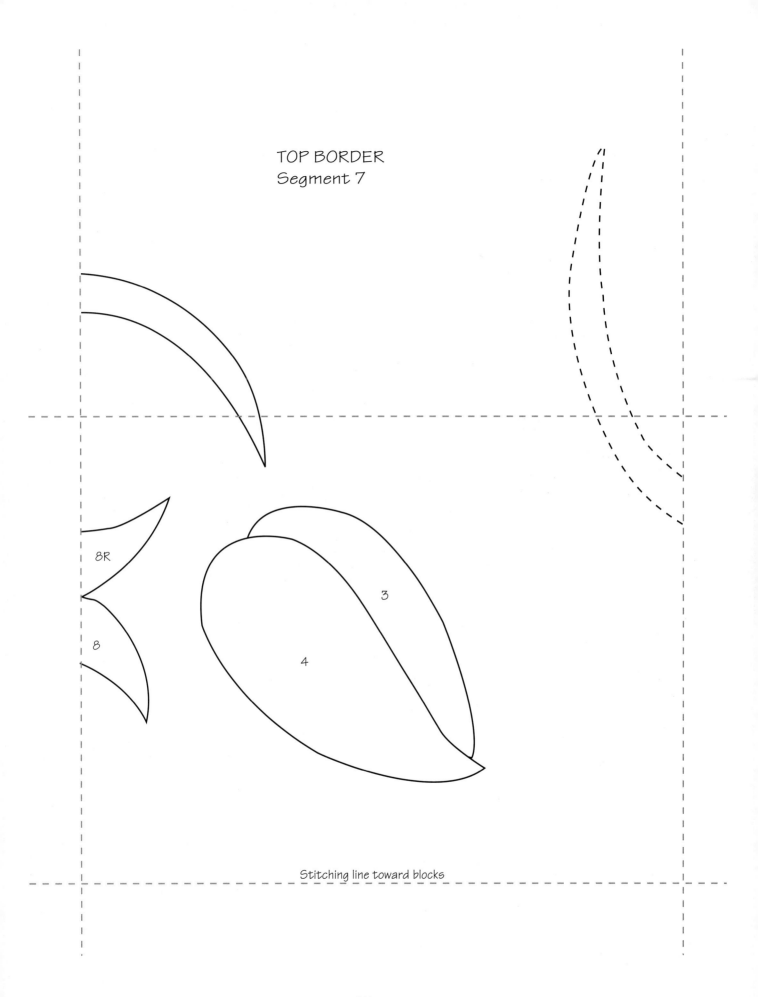

TOP BORDER
Segment 7

8R

8

3

4

Stitching line toward blocks

141

TOP BORDER
Segment 8

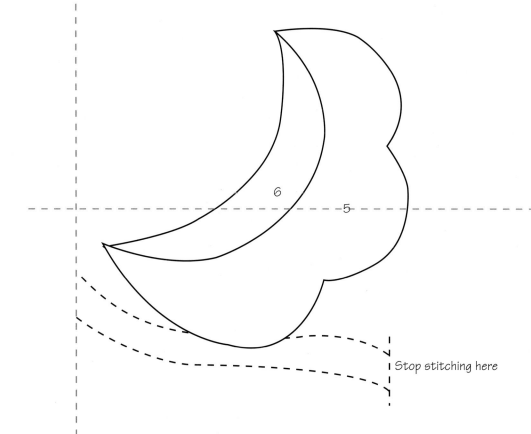

6

5

Stop stitching here

Stitching line toward blocks

Stitching line toward blocks

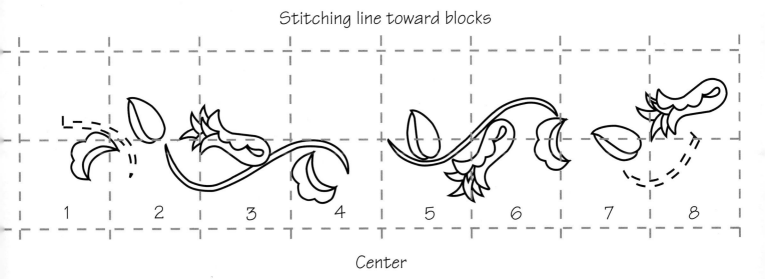

1   2   3   4   5   6   7   8

Center

EXOTICA- BOTTOM BORDER
Stitched by Pat Campbell, Dallas, Texas

BOTTOM BORDER
Segment 1

Stitching line toward blocks

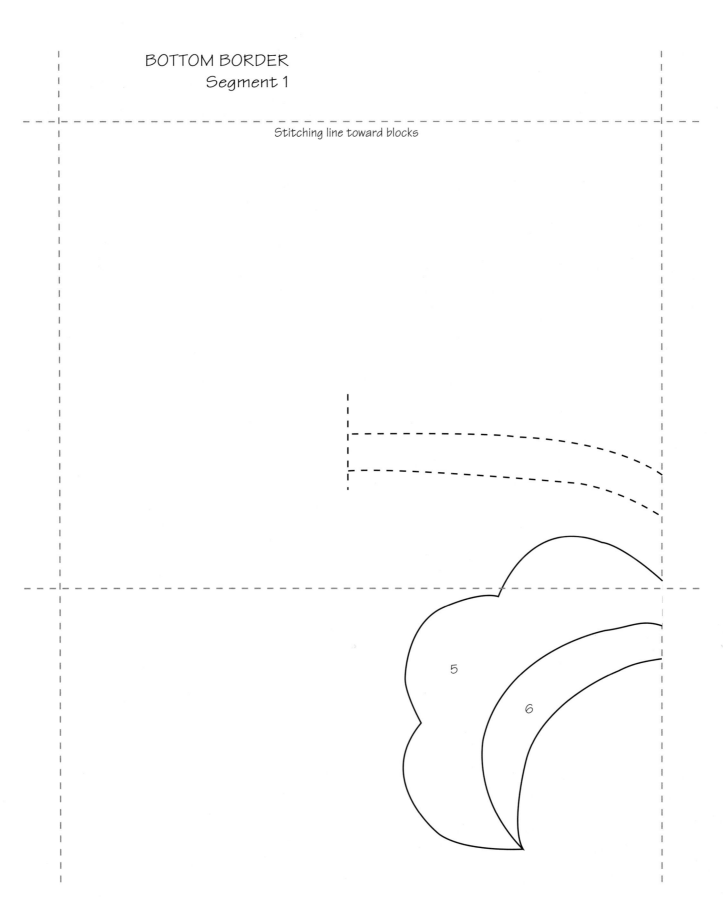

5

6

144

Stitching line toward blocks

BOTTOM BORDER
Segment 2

3

4

8

14

14

BOTTOM BORDER
Segment 3

BOTTOM BORDER
Segment 4

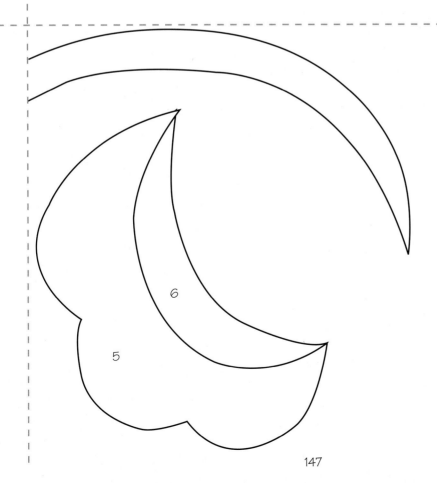

5

6

BOTTOM BORDER
Segment 5

Center line

3

4

7R

8

14

Stitching line toward blocks

BOTTOM BORDER
Segment 6

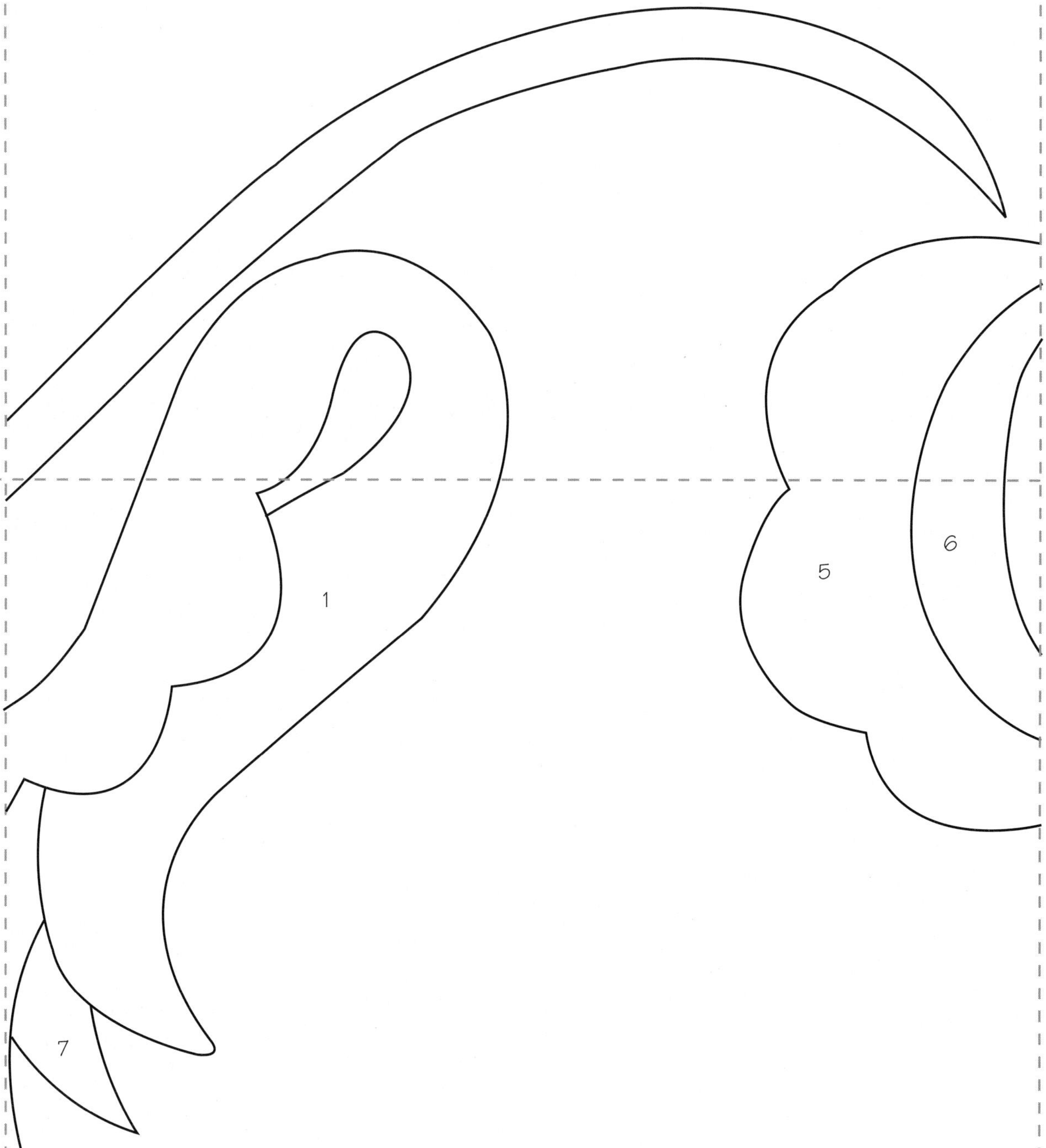

1

5

6

7

BOTTOM BORDER
Segment 7

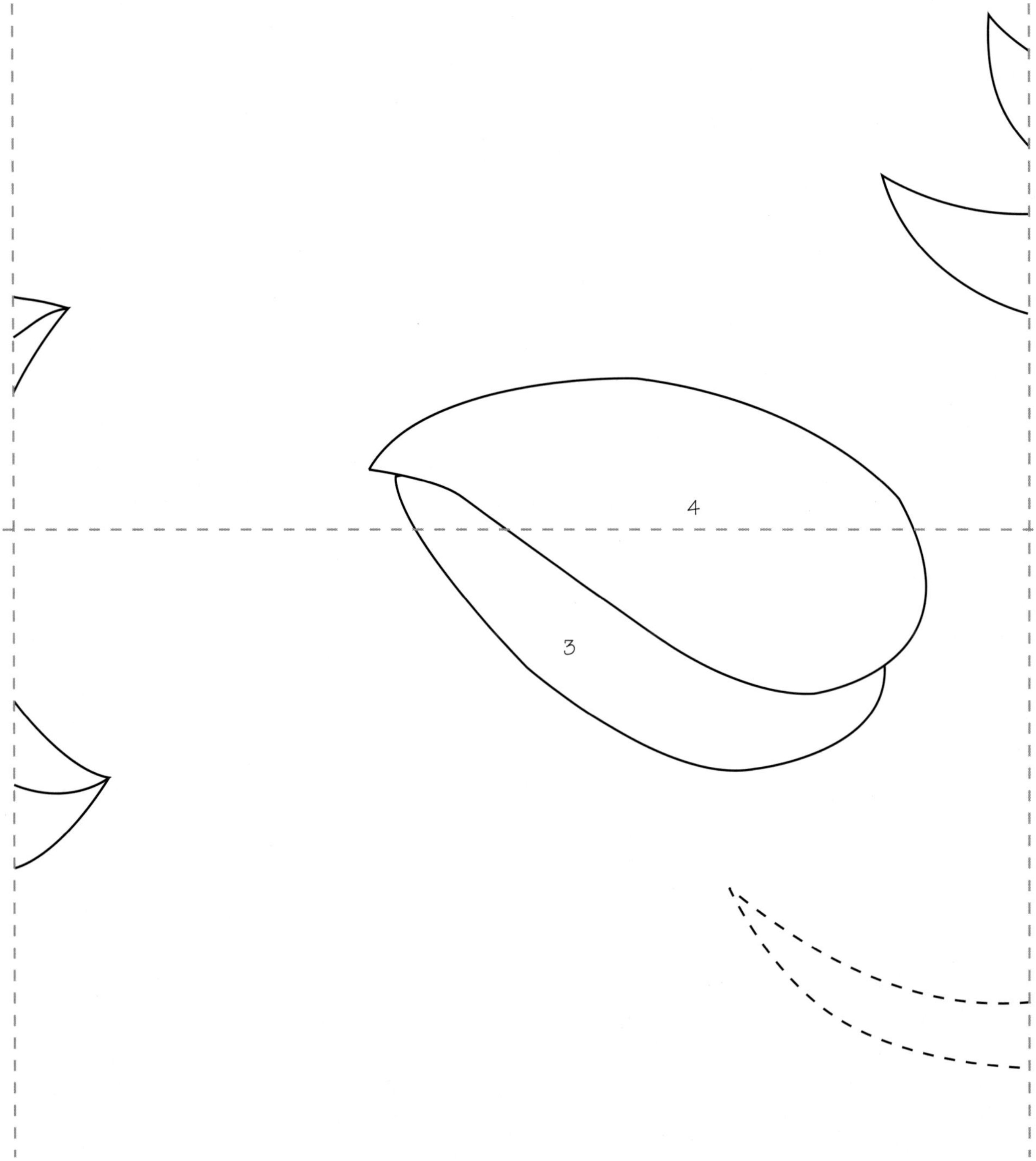

4

3

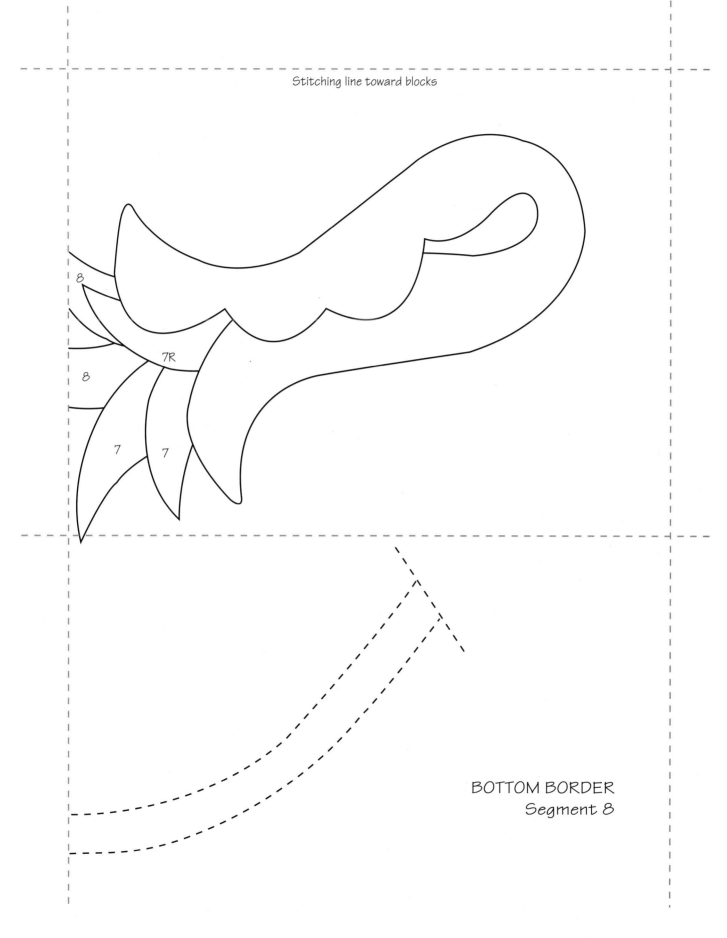

Stitching line toward blocks

BOTTOM BORDER
Segment 8

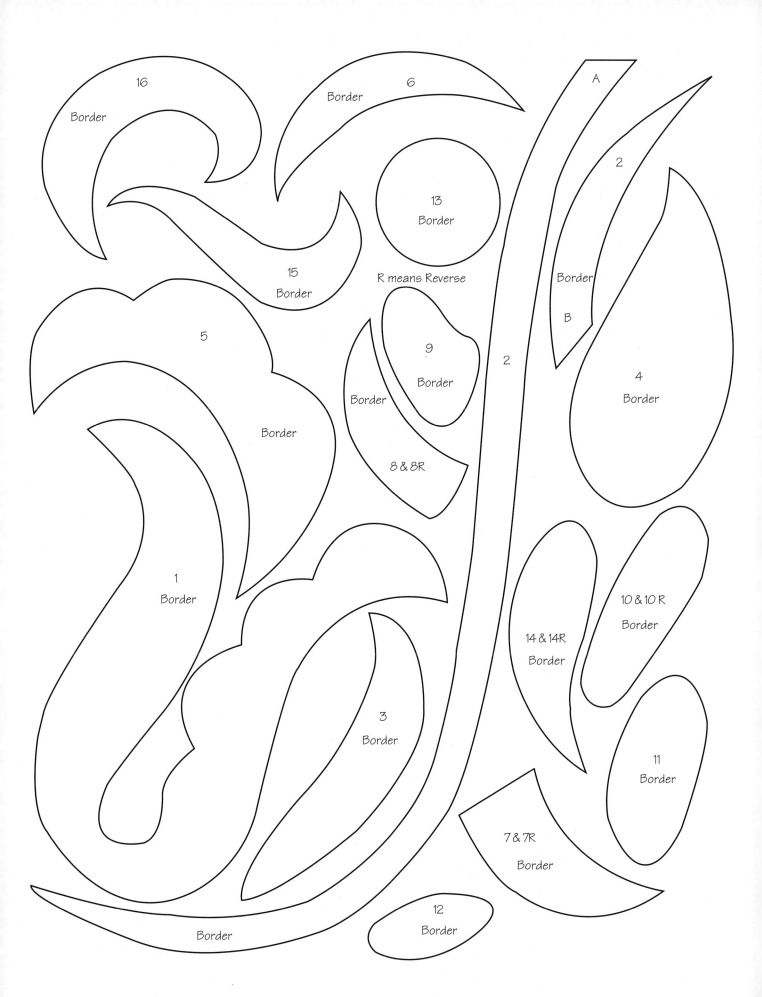

16
Border

Border
6

13
Border

2

15
Border

R means Reverse

B
Border

A

5

9
Border

4
Border

Border

Border

8 & 8R

2

1
Border

10 & 10 R
Border

14 & 14R
Border

3
Border

11
Border

7 & 7R
Border

Border

12
Border

EXOTICA- BORDER CORNER ALIGNMENT
TOP ROW: Alignment of side borders with top border.
BOTOM ROW: Alignment of side borders with bottom border.

Q&A

ANSWERS TO THE QUESTIONS MOST OFTEN ASKED

Q. What makes a Jacobean quilt different from other quilts?

A. The most important characteristic is that they reflect the style of a specific era – 17th century crewel embroidery. They are usually hung rather than used on beds. A wide rather than a limited palette of colors and fantasy rather than realism are practiced. Stitches are hidden rather than employed to enchance the design.

Q. Should I always use only cotton fabric?

A. Cotton is the easiest fabric to work with, but try others. Silk tends to flatten and to deteriorate; blends frustrate the maker; linen and wool are heavy; rayon is hard to needle turn.

Q. How do I know if a piece of fabric in my collection is 100% cotton?

A. Snip off a small piece, put it in an ashtray and set it on fire. If ashes of the "blow away" type remain, it's 100% cotton. Any other reaction, for example, melting, indicates that other fibers are present in your fabric.

Q. Is the tree trunk always only one fabric?

A. It can be or you can use several fabrics, if you like.

Q. Can I use plain colored fabric for the appliqué?

A. Solids tend to be flat/dead. If you decide to use solids, don't use just one or two patterned calicoes with them. It would be better to introduce one or two solids to many two-toned calicoes.

Q. Should I wash and iron my fabrics?

A. Only if they're for a gift quilt or a baby quilt. Otherwise, its unnecessary. Many quiltmakers no longer spend time doing a job they don't really want to do but were told they should do. A quilt used as a wallhanging will get soiled, but you can have it dry cleaned. Do what feels right for you.

Q. What seam allowance do I use?

A. ⅛" on all design pieces and ¼" on all the seams in the blocks, borders, binding, and sleeve.

Q. Do I need to baste?

A. Only large pieces. They can be pin basted with sequin pins placed on the wrong side. Don't hesitate to thread baste rather than pin baste, however, if it makes you more confident.

Q. Which piece do I appliqué first?

A. Start with the tree trunk, which is usually your biggest piece.

Q. Where do I start stitching?

A. On a gentle curve. Never start at a point.

Q. Must I use a small needle?

A. There are no "musts," but since only ⅓ of the needle is needed for needle turn, why use a longer one, which will be more to push through the fabric?

Q. Why can't I use my needle instead of a quilting pin for the "perfect point?"

A. The quilting pin is stronger and will do a better job.

Q. Should I clip the curve of a design piece?

A. You'll need to clip the curve of a "U" and the point of the deep "V." Otherwise, it is rarely necessary, because your seam allowance is narrow (⅛" instead of the usual ¼"). You'll feel a drag on the needle, or the fabric fold will unfold when you need to clip. Never clip circles.

Q. Must I stitch through all the fabric layers?

A. It's not necessary.

Q. What if the design piece frays; for example, at the point?

A. Don't think of it as "fray." Consider the remaining threads the seam allowance, and tuck them under with your needle.

Q. What if a dark design piece placed under a light design piece shows through?

A. Make a slip for it. Cut a piece of voile, organza, or organdy the same shape as your template (no added seam allowance) and sandwich it between the dark and the light.

Q. What if a fabric thread pokes out?

A. When a thread does that a good description is: it "eeks" out – "eek" as in the cartoon where the character with her hair standing on end climbs on a chair and squeals, "Eek! A mouse!" Students have the same reaction with these threads that poke their noses out. Relax and with your needle push the thread(s) back in.

Q. What lamp is best?

A. A gooseneck table lamp works well for trying out fabrics and laying out pieces. A pendant lamp helps for stitching. Make sure the light bulb wattage is high enough for you to be able to see well.

Q. Do I cut away the background fabric from behind the design after I finish appliquéing?

A. Don't trim away the background fabric. Jacobean quilts are usually hung. Pulling, tugging and hanging are hard on them. However, it's not wrong. The English don't drive on the wrong side of the road; they drive on the other side of the road. Remember: choose what you like from your teachers and do as you please.

Q. Do I cut out all the pieces for the block before I start to stitch?

A. Yes. Cut pieces for one block before you begin to stitch, but you do not have to cut all the pieces for all the blocks.

THE STITCHERS

Block 1
GRACE SOHN
ESSEX, CONNECTICUT
Grandmother, extensive traveler, gardener, boater, antique collector.
"As my husband and I traveled through Europe I admired the medieval tapestries and Jacobean embroideries that were in so many of the castles and museums. In this ten-year period of vacation and business travel I was busy sewing baby quilts and then twin-size quilts for 12 grandchildren. Now it's time to spend all my quilting time on Jacobean appliqué."

Block 2
ROSLYN HAY
AUSTRALIA
Quilt teacher, optimist, artist, dreamer, historian, mother, giver.
"Needlework has been an important part of my life since I was eight, or maybe even before then. I feel fortunate to be talented in this field and thankful I am able to share everything I know with others, plus leave a legacy for all to enjoy."

Block 3
MICHELLE JACK
GARLAND, TEXAS
Single career woman.
"I have a busy career and a small business on the side. Quilting is an outlet for my creative juices and a great stress reliever. With an extensive background in art, quilting allows me the vehicle to paint without a brush and canvas."

Block 4
SHARON CHAMBERS
MESQUITE, TEXAS
Quiltmaker, homemaker, field interviewer for Census Bureau.
"I find that the Jacobean appliqué allows more freedom in fabric use and color than other appliqué styles; i.e., Baltimore Album."

Block 5
MAUREEN A. CARLSON
MOLINE, ILLINOIS
Seamstress, mother, gourmet cook, traveler, decorator (of her own new home).
"I've been quilting for almost ten years with the last two years focusing on appliqué. I enjoy collecting old quilts and unfinished tops. I call these 'rescues' (someone has to care for them). I always take an appliqué project along when we travel to keep myself busy."

Block 6
JENNIFER PATRIARCHE
REDMOND, WASHINGTON
Quiltmaker, quilt teacher (both appliqué and rotary cutting/machine piecing), traveler, ex-nurse.
"Quilting to me is a wonderful opportunity to interpret my life and the world around me using color, design, and texture. As well, quilting has provided me with friendship and fun. I am very proud to be part of this book."

Block 7
NANCY J. STEIDLE
SANTA FE, NEW MEXICO
Quiltmaker, wife, stepmother, entrepreneur, avid reader, gardener, hiker.
"Quilts, quiltmaking, and quilters have been a great influence on my life for the past 13 years. Each quilter I've met has added a new dimension to my approach. Having always been an avid piecer and a stickler for quality workmanship, I was intrigued with Pat Campbell's methods in Jacobean appliqué."

Block 8
GAIL KESSLER
OLEY, PENNSYLVANIA
Appliqué teacher, mother, wife, gardener, Pennsylvania Dutch farm-girl-at-heart.
An appliqué/fabricholic's dream come true, Pat's classy Jacobean designs are a wonderful way to combine seventeenth century elegance with the bold, rich drama of today's fabrics. I love all types of appliqué — but Pat's designs? They make me grab those special fabrics I've been saving up on the top shelf."

Block 9
SALLY ASHBACHER
ROWLETT, TEXAS
Wife, mother, grandmother, small business owner, fashion retailer, published quiltmaker, licensed realtor, Tea Room cook, and quilt teacher.
"My earliest memories of needlework are learning embroidery at my mother's knee after morning kindergarten. We progressed together through cross stitch, crewel, needlepoint, and dressmaking. If she were alive today, I know we'd be quilting! My pas-

sion is colorful, pieced scrap quilts. However, since taking appliqué from Pat and learning her precision techniques, I could come to have a dual passion."

Right Border
JOANNA (THOMASON) SHAMPINE
RICHARDSON, TEXAS
Wife, mother, friend, learner, doer.
"It was a pleasure to appliqué the beautiful fabrics that were used in a lovely pattern. Doing the Jacobean appliqué sharpened my sewing skills and taught me about designing appliqué patterns."

Left Border
STEPHANIE J. BRASKEY
POTTSTOWN, PENNSYLVANIA
Mother, mathematician and programmer/analyst-systems engineer, stitcher, painter, cook, carpenter (my husband and I built our own home - a colonial reproduction).
"Being mother to four sons is my primary interest and responsi-

bility, but quiltmaking is my 'sanctuary.' Everyone needs a sanctuary – a time and/or place to be alone and do what one loves to do most, to let our thoughts and creativity flow freely. Quiltmaking, especially appliqué, is that 'sanctuary' for me."

Top and Bottom Borders
PAT CAMPBELL, DALLAS, TEXAS

Quilting
THEKLA SCHNITKER, HOYLETON, ILLINOIS

Marking of Quilting Design
ETHEL MARIE HAFER, DALLAS, TEXAS

Pattern Drafting
THERESA WITTER, DALLAS, TEXAS

Figures
MIMI AYARS, BEDFORD, TEXAS

Also Thanks to
LINDA BALLOU, LIVERMORE, CALIFORNIA

PREFERRED PRODUCTS

Fabric
    Background fabric -
        Gutcheon's "American Classic"
    Design fabric - RJR
        Alexander Henry
        Hoffman
        Skydyes

Thread
    Mettler #60 Machine Embroidery
    DMC #50 Machine Embroidery

Scissors
    Fiskars® 5" Sharp Point
    Gingher® 4" Embroidery

Needles
    Clover #12 Betweens

Pencils
    Berol™ Prisma Color®
    Veri Thin®

Eraser
    Pentel Clic®

Pens
    Sharpie®
    Pigma®

Batting
    Hobbs "Thermore"
    Hobbs "Polydown"

Quilt Frame
    The Flynn Quilt Frame
    Morgan Craft Stand

Neither Pat Campbell nor Mimi Ayars represents any of the companies who make the products suggested in this book. The recommended items, however, have been tested by them and found to be consistently of high quality and reliability.

ABOUT THE AUTHORS

Patricia B. Campbell, born and reared in Michigan, makes her home in Dallas, Texas. An award-winning applique artist, she is well-known as an exciting speaker and an inspiring instructor. She has adapted 17th and 18th century Jacobean designs from embroidery to fabric and has created a line of original patterns for sale. She has taught workshops from Indianapolis, Indiana to Port Elizabeth, South Africa. Her first quilt "Jacobean Arbor" — a well-known and beloved black quilt — won 8 ribbons, including a Best of Show. It was followed by "Elizabethan Woods', a five-time ribbon winner. She and her quilts have appeared on the covers and been featured in articles in *American Quilter*, Summer, 1990 and Fall, 1991; *International Quilt Festival*, Fall/Winter, 1991; and *Quilting Today*, 1991; and *Patchwork Quilt Tsuchin*, 1991; *Quilting International*, July, 1992.

A native of Delaware, Mimi Ayars, Ph.D., calls herself a "hardy Texas transplant." She caught the spirit of quilting in the 1976 revival, while living in the Chicago area. Once she belonged to five guild simultaneously. Her first quilt, "Stars and Stripes," was selected for a show of bicentennial quilts at the Museum of the American Quilting Society in 1991.

Dr. Ayars has taught sociology at nine Universities in six states. She retired in 1991 to pursue two hobbies: writing and quilting. Quilt articles by her have been published in the *National Quilting Association's Quilting Quarterly* (former *Patchwork Patter*) and *Quilt World*.

"I am a piecer, not a patcher," she says, "but if anyone could convert me, it would be Pat Campbell."

~American Quilter's Society~

dedicated to publishing books for today's quilters

The following AQS publications are currently available:

- **Adapting Architectural Details for Quilts,** Carol Wagner, #2282: AQS, 1991, 88 pages, $12.95
- **American Beauties: Rose & Tulip Quilts,** Gwen Marston & Joe Cunningham, #1907: AQS, 1988, 96 pages, $14.95
- **America's Pictorial Quilts,** Caron L. Mosey, #1662: AQS, 1985, 112 pages, hardbound, $19.95
- **Applique Designs: My Mother Taught Me to Sew,** Faye Anderson, #2121: AQS, 1990, 80 pages, $12.95
- **Arkansas Quilts: Arkansas Warmth,** Arkansas Quilter's Guild, Inc., #1908: AQS, 1987, 144 pages, hardbound, $24.95
- **The Art of Hand Applique,** Laura Lee Fritz, #2122: AQS, 1990, 80 pages, $14.95
- **...Ask Helen More About Quilting Designs,** Helen Squire, #2099: AQS, 1990, 54 pages, 17 x 11, spiral-bound, $14.95
- **Award-Winning Quilts & Their Makers: Vol. I, The Best of AQS Shows – 1985-1987,** #2207: AQS, 1991, 232 pages, $24.95
- **Award-Winning Quilts & Their Makers: Vol. II, The Best of AQS Shows – 1988-1989,** #2354: AQS, 1992, 176 pages, $24.95
- **Award-Winning Quilts & Their Makers: Vol. III, The Best of AQS Shows – 1990-1991,** #3425: AQS, 1993, 180 pages, $24.95
- **Classic Basket Quilts,** Elizabeth Porter & Marianne Fons, #2208: AQS, 1991, 128 pages, $16.95
- **A Collection of Favorite Quilts,** Judy Florence, #2119: AQS, 1990, 136 pages, $18.95
- **Creative Machine Art,** Sharee Dawn Roberts, #2355: AQS, 1992, 142 pages, 9 x 9, $24.95
- **Dear Helen, Can You Tell Me?...all about quilting designs,** Helen Squire, #1820: AQS, 1987, 51 pages, 17 x 11, spiral-bound, $12.95
- **Dye Painting!,** Ann Johnston, #3399: AQS, 1992, 88 pages, $19.95
- **Dyeing & Overdyeing of Cotton Fabrics,** Judy Mercer Tescher, #2030: AQS, 1990, 54 pages, $9.95
- **Flavor Quilts for Kids to Make: Complete Instructions for Teaching Children to Dye, Decorate & Sew Quilts,** Jennifer Amor #2356: AQS, 1991, 120 pages, $12.95
- **From Basics to Binding: A Complete Guide to Making Quilts,** Karen Kay Buckley, #2381: AQS, 1992, 160 pages, $16.95
- **Fun & Fancy Machine Quiltmaking,** Lois Smith, #1982: AQS, 1989, 144 pages, $19.95
- **Gallery of American Quilts 1830-1991: Book III,** #3421: AQS, 1992, 128 pages, $19.95
- **The Grand Finale: A Quilter's Guide to Finishing Projects,** Linda Denner, #1924: AQS, 1988, 96 pages, $14.95
- **Heirloom Miniatures,** Tina M. Gravatt, #2097: AQS, 1990, 64 pages, $9.95
- **Infinite Stars,** Gayle Bong, #2283: AQS, 1992, 72 pages, $12.95
- **The Ins and Outs: Perfecting the Quilting Stitch,** Patricia J. Morris, #2120: AQS, 1990, 96 pages, $9.95
- **Irish Chain Quilts: A Workbook of Irish Chains & Related Patterns,** Joyce B. Peaden, #1906: AQS, 1988, 96 pages, $14.95
- **The Log Cabin Returns to Kentucky: Quilts from the Pilgrim/Roy Collection,** Gerald Roy and Paul Pilgrim, #3329: AQS, 1992, 36 pages, 9 x 7, $12.95
- **Marbling Fabrics for Quilts: A Guide for Learning & Teaching,** Kathy Fawcett & Carol Shoaf, #2206: AQS, 1991, 72 pages, $12.95
- **More Projects and Patterns: A Second Collection of Favorite Quilts,** Judy Florence, #3330: AQS, 1992, 152 pages, $18.95
- **Nancy Crow: Quilts and Influences,** Nancy Crow, #1981: AQS, 1990, 256 pages, 9 x 12, hardcover, $29.95
- **Nancy Crow: Work in Transition,** Nancy Crow, #3331: AQS, 1992, 32 pages, 9 x 10, $12.95
- **New Jersey Quilts – 1777 to 1950: Contributions to an American Tradition,** The Heritage Quilt Project of New Jersey; text by Rachel Cochran, Rita Erickson, Natalie Hart & Barbara Schaffer, #3332: AQS, 1992, 256 pages, $29.95
- **No Dragons on My Quilt,** Jean Ray Laury with Ritva Laury & Lizabeth Laury, #2153: AQS, 1990, 52 pages, hardcover, $12.95
- **Oklahoma Heritage Quilts,** Oklahoma Quilt Heritage Project #2032: AQS, 1990, 144 pages, $19.95
- **Old Favorites in Miniature,** Tina M. Gravatt, #3469: AQS, 1993, 104 pages, $15.95.
- **Quilt Groups Today: Who They Are, Where They Meet, What They Do, and How to Contact Them; A Complete Guide for 1992-1993,** #3308: AQS, 1992, 336 pages, $14.95
- **Quilting Patterns from Native American Designs,** Dr. Joyce Mori, #3467: AQS, 1993, 80 pages, $12.95
- **Quilting with Style: Principles for Great Pattern Design,** Gwen Marston & Joe Cunningham, #3470: AQS, 1993, 192 pages, 9" x 12", hardcover, $24.95.
- **Quiltmaker's Guide: Basics & Beyond,** Carol Doak, #2284: AQS, 1992, 208 pages, $19.95
- **Quilts: Old & New, A Similar View,** Paul D. Pilgrim and Gerald E. Roy, #3715: AQS, 1993, 40 pages, $12.95
- **Quilts: The Permanent Collection – MAQS,** #2257: AQS, 1991, 100 pages, 10 x 6½, $9.95
- **Sensational Scrap Quilts,** Darra Duffy Williamson, #2357: AQS, 1992, 152 pages, $24.95
- **Show Me Helen...How to Use Quilting Designs,** Helen Squire, #3375: AQS, 1993, 155 pages, $15.95
- **Sets & Borders,** Gwen Marston & Joe Cunningham, #1821: AQS, 1987, 104 pages, $14.95
- **Somewhere in Between: Quilts and Quilters of Illinois,** Rita Barrow Barber, #1790: AQS, 1986, 78 pages, $14.95
- **Stenciled Quilts for Christmas,** Marie Monteith Sturmer, #2098: AQS, 1990, 104 pages, $14.95
- **A Treasury of Quilting Designs,** Linda Goodmon Emery, #2029: AQS, 1990, 80 pages, 14 x 11, spiral-bound, $14.95
- **Wonderful Wearables: A Celebration of Creative Clothing,** Virginia Avery, #2286: AQS, 1991, 184 pages, $24.95

These books can be found in local bookstores and quilt shops. If you are unable to locate a title in your area, you can order by mail from AQS, P.O. Box 3290, Paducah, KY 42002-3290. Please add $1 for the first book and 40¢ for each additional one to cover postage and handling. (International orders please add $1.50 for the first book and $1 for each additional one.)